YOU PROMISED
WHEN THE
WAR ENDED…

YOU PROMISED WHEN THE WAR ENDED...

HENRIETTA ROWANSFORDE
ILLUSTRATED BY THE AUTHOR

Order this book online at www.trafford.com
or email orders@trafford.com

Most Trafford titles are also available at major online book retailers.

Note for Librarians: A cataloguing record for this book is available from Library
and Archives Canada at www.collectionscanada.ca/amicus/index-e.html

Printed in Victoria, BC, Canada.

ISBN: 978-1-4251-9011-8 (sc)
ISBN: 978-1-4269-1093-7 (hc)
ISBN: 978-1-4269-1148-4 (eb)

*Our mission is to efficiently provide the world's finest, most comprehensive book publishing
service, enabling every author to experience success. To find out how to publish your book, your
way, and have it available worldwide, visit us online at www.trafford.com*

Trafford rev. 10/09/09

 www.trafford.com

North America & international
toll-free: 1 888 232 4444 (USA & Canada)
phone: 250 383 6864 ♦ fax: 812 355 4082

This book is dedicated to my parents, to our family Nanny,
to all my brothers and sisters, including those
born after the end of the book and
to Mike, our children and our grandchildren

Acknowledgements

Heartfelt thanks to all my many friends who have
encouraged me in this endeavour;
you all know who you are!

Author's Note

I wrote the original draft entirely based on recollections of
my life when I was four and five years old. I then presented it to
my brothers and sisters who read the manuscript and seemed to
enjoy the account of our family life during those years.

All the family members, including Nanny of course, and
the animals are/were real. All other characters are figments of
my imagination. The story is based on actual events as I recall
them.

Preface

I was conceived, my Mother once told me (in an unusually frank conversation) the night before my father left to fight in World War II.

The day I was born he was missing in action, and by the time my mother was notified that he had escaped from Dunkirk and had arrived safely back in England, I was sixteen days old.

Thus began my life.

I have written this book as I remember those turbulent years and I trust that I have been able to convey the manner in which, although we lived in the country away from the blitz and the bombing, the War permeated many aspects of our lives. Threaded through this story of scarcity and lack are my mother's exotic tales of romance and love in earlier, happier times.

This book is also a testimony to the strength and courage with which Mother and Nanny brought us children safely and lovingly through those tempestuous years.

Chapter 1
The Adventure Begins

"Nanny, I'm frightened." With tears in my eyes I think about moving far, far away to a village I have never heard of, leaving my home, my very own garden and everything I know behind.

"No, Henrietta, you mustn't be frightened," she says, firmly, "you're a big girl now you are four. Your mother says that Upper Nettlebourne is a very nice village and the new house has a much larger garden. She says that we will all love living there. Felicity is going to help you start your new garden so she has dug up your evening primrose roots and put them in a box together with your mother's daffodil bulbs. And, before you ask, yes, I do have all your drawings so that we can put some up in the new nursery."

"I still don't want to go!" I stamp my foot angrily.

"Don't you stamp your foot at me, young lady," Nan says, sounding annoyed. "You are behaving like a spoilt child, and I don't like spoilt children do I? There is nothing to worry about, just think of this as a big adventure." As usual, her voice calms me down and I try to change the subject in my head when I suddenly remember, with horror, something very important indeed.

"Oh! What about Pippa? Can you dig her up for me?"

She replies rather sharply that, no, she can't dig her up. "She is happy where she is and you've seen how well the pansies we planted on her grave have grown."

"I can't leave my baby behind!"

"Henny, she will be safe and happy here, and I am sure that the next little girl to live in this house will look after the pansies for you. I know that you feel worried and I expect that you have tummy ache?" I nod.

"Yes, I thought you might have. Every time you get upset it hurts, doesn't it? Why don't I get you a few of the jammy bits from the tin of broken biscuits? Will that make you feel better?" I smile at her and Nan goes off to the kitchen and returns with a saucer-full. "Now, just calm down. I promise you that everything will be all right."

"Nan, Hugh says there will be bombs…"

"Oh! What nonsense! Whatever next? I will have to have a word with that young man. How naughty of your brother to tell you bad things like that, no wonder you are unhappy. Everything will be all right, I promise.

"Now, come on, we need to finish packing all the toys in this last tea chest. Cheer up, Henny," She hands me my best friend, Ted. He is the teddy bear that she knitted especially for me just before I was born as her present to welcome me into the world.

"Tomorrow we start on our big adventure but now it is time for me to give Elizabeth her supper. Why don't you and Ted

go up and see if you can see any parachutes?"

We climb up onto the chair that Nan leaves on the landing half way up the stairs for us and watch as flocks of beautiful coloured parachutes float down to earth. When there are no more in the sky we go back downstairs`to Nan in the nursery.

Mother suddenly arrives with a bundle of clothes in her arms. "Look what I found under Hugo's bed, Nan, all those school shirts of his that we couldn't find. There is no time to wash them before we leave so we will have to pack them as they are and wash them at the new place; what a nuisance."

Nan says that she will see to them and asks if she can please tell me a story whilst she attends to the baby. "I have a bottle ready for her; she's been so restless today that I think it will help settle her." Elizabeth, drinks her milk contentedly, quite unaware that our whole life is about to change dramatically.

"Once upon a time there was a beautiful young lady," Mother begins, modestly describing herself, "who lived by the sea with her father and mother, her sisters and her nanny. One fine spring day she received an invitation from the Commanding Officer to a Ball at the Officer's Mess in the Castle, which was set high up on a hill above the town.

"My mother, your grandmother, decided that I should have a new ball gown, so we went downtown to the draper's shop where we bought yards of pale blue crêpe-de-chine and to the haberdasher's where we bought yards of lace trim. That afternoon the seamstress started creating the gown. I had a stylish pair of silver shoes and a long string of pearls to wear with it. Your grandmother promised that she would lend me her ostrich feather fan with the ivory handle."

She sees that I am about to interrupt her. "Yes, that is the one that is now in the summer trunk." She makes herself more comfortable and presses on with the story. "The next day the gown was finished and I knew that I would look very beautiful wearing it.

"My father, your grandfather, was a very old fashioned doctor who still went on his rounds in his horse-drawn carriage. He said that he would arrange for me to be driven up to the Castle and would escort me to the receiving line. Secretly, I would rather have arrived in one of the modern dashing coupés."

"What's a 'coopay'?" I enquire.

"It's a type of car with a roof that folds down like the pram hood. Now it is getting late, so we will finish the story another night."

"Oh, please, please tell me about the Ball," I beg. "Ted really wants to hear about it, don't you, Ted?"

"No, Henrietta, you should not have interrupted me. Off to bed now. We have a very exciting day ahead of us tomorrow."

Chapter 2
My Family

Our father, the Colonel, is somebody important in the Army and, I'm not sure, but I think he lives in the desert. I have never met him, but Mother, who always refers to him as her Beloved, says that he has blue eyes and is a kind, handsome, brave man.

Mother is the tallest in the family and, like the rest of us has hazel eyes and black hair (except for the Little One who has golden fluff). She wears her long hair piled on top of her head or swept up and held in place with tortoiseshell combs. Her skin is very soft and she smells of eau de Cologne and her face powder. She is proud of the fact that she is slim although she has had five children; the four of us, and Darling Hilary. There is a photo beside her bed of her holding a large baby and she told Felicity, my big sister, who told me, that the baby Hilary had been too perfect to live, so she died. This happened long before I was born and we are never allowed to mention her.

Sometimes, if Mother's nerves are bad, she vanishes; I might wake up one morning and I can't find her anywhere. Nan says that she goes to stay with one of her sisters and when she feels happier she will return home again. Of course I miss her when she disappears, but I do feel very safe with Nan and Ted and we always have such a happy time together. For some reason, Hugo, my big brother, whom I call Hugh, helps Nan a lot more and is kinder to me and my baby sister when our mother is not here.

Mother is very artistic and dramatic and tells me that she would prefer to wear big hats and long, flowing clothes, however, due to the Wartime clothes rationing, she has to make do with plain frocks with short skirts. She really loves the gypsies and has said more than once that she wishes that she could wander around England in a horse-drawn caravan, dressed in long, striped skirts over full petticoats, with a big shawl, gold hoop earrings and her hair plaited and tied in loops the way they do.

She is a wonderful storyteller and when she is happy her face shines and she is very excited, and exciting, and has lots of good ideas about things we can do and make.

My big sister Felicity says that she is ten years older than me. She is tall and slim and is almost a Grown-Up. She is very clever and reads and studies a lot and says she loves 'xams', whatever they are. She especially enjoys her History lessons at her school in Patisford. She helps Nan with the cooking and she can draw, but only owls. Sometimes she plays with us when she is not busy. She says that she will grow lots of vegetables for us all and maybe some fruit and flowers at the new house. When I ask her if I can help her with the gardening she says that I can as long as I do what she tells me.

Hugh thinks he's very important because he's ten years old. Nan says that he is very wild and he says that he hates school. He tells me that he can boss me around because he is the Man of the Family until our father returns. When he grows up he wants to be a soldier or a boxer. I want to be a boxer like him too when I grow up. In summertime Mother and I go to watch him play in school cricket matches on the Abbey Pasture in Patisford.

Nan came to help Mother three weeks before I was born. She told me that she planned to leave when I was three weeks old to look after another newborn. However, she loved me, the new baby, so much that she could not leave and so stayed to look after us all. Before she came to us, she had been Nanny to the McPherson children, who lived in London and who had all been extremely well behaved.

She is sort of plump, like me, and not as tall as Mother and she always wears a uniform, a hair net to keep her brown hair tidy in the daytime and she puts twisty brown curlers in her hair at night. She has blue eyes and wears gold-rimmed spectacles when she reads to me or when she sews.

One rainy afternoon she told me a terrible story about what happened when she was little. It was a bitterly cold winter and she and her sister, Tabitha, became so ill that, one frosty night, they were sent to hospital in a horse-drawn ambulance. The horses galloped as fast as they possibly could but they did not reach the hospital in time. Holding Nan's hand, Tabitha died. Nan has never, ever been ill since that dreadful day.

Her morning frocks are either blue or dark pink with soft white collars and cuffs and she wears a soft white apron. After lunch, she goes upstairs to change and we are not allowed to disturb her unless there is a Drama. She eventually comes downstairs dressed in her grey frock with starched white collar and cuffs and a big white starched apron with wide straps that cross over at the back. Every afternoon she removes her apron, puts on her grey hat, and her coat, if it is cold, and takes us for long walks pushing our old pram, which Hugh has painted grey to match Nan.

She says that I am big for my age but very clumsy because I keep tripping over my feet. After brushing my long hair each morning, she either ties it up in bunches or plaits it for me. I like getting up in the morning but I hate going to bed because I often sleep badly.

The Little One, Elizabeth, or Lizzybuff, as I call her, is my small sister, who, Nan says, is eighteen months old. We call her the Dormouse because she sleeps a lot curled up in a ball. She is getting a bit more interesting as she grows bigger and she talks a lot but I don't know what about because Nan says it's not 'Nglish it's gobbledegook.

Nan is always the same, very kind and comforting, and I know that she loves me whatever I do and that she will keep me safe from all my fears and from my brother. She is also a very good cook, which is lucky, because Mother only makes fancy things like cakes and puddings.

Lloyd is our batman* and I like him very much. I am sad that we have to leave him behind to look after the next family in our old house.

Our lady cat's name is Clementina. She is a tortoiseshell cat. Her fur coat is mainly white with patches of black, white and ginger; she has big yellow eyes, a pink nose and a long stripey tail. She likes to sit by the fire in the winter watching the sparks fly up the chimney and in the summer she chases butterflies but never catches any.

Poor Old Bunker is our black and white spaniel; he and I are not close friends. He belongs to our father and I think that he misses him a lot because he is always so miserable.

* A batman is a soldier assigned to a commissioned officer as a personal servant

Chapter 3
Moving Day

"When we arrive at the new house we'll have a picnic lunch with a special treat for us all," Nan says. "I want you to be very good and quiet today, Henny, because your mother's nerves aren't very good."

I know that can mean trouble; dear Nan, she always warns me.

"Will our father know where we've moved to when he comes back at the end of the War?" I enquire, anxiously.

"Of course, Henny, he helped your mother choose the new house …"

"Then why didn't he come to see us?"

Her patience finally snaps. "Now, Henrietta, stop asking questions, you are getting over-excited. Your father was far too busy to visit us and he is now on his way back to his posting. I want you to sit down and be quiet for five minutes while I finish feeding Elizabeth, and then we will pack the last few things." Ted and I sit as quiet as we can be and wonder what it will be like riding in the army lorry.

Moving day finally arrives and Felicity and Hugh go to Patisford on the bus with a picnic lunch because there will not be enough room for them to travel in the army lorry. Hugh is going up to the railway station to collect train numbers and Felicity is going to do some shopping and then she will spend the morning in the second hand bookshop near the market. She says she will eat her lunch on a bench in the Abbey Gardens and then read until it is time to meet Hugh at the bus station. They will catch the bus and arrive at the new house in time for supper.

"The lorry is here, Nan," Mother announces. "Lloyd is helping the soldiers load our beds and bedding and the few remaining items that we needed last night. I am thankful that they put most of our things in yesterday. Yes, Henrietta, of course, we won't forget the animals."

The big lorry is already jam-packed with our furniture and other things including the box of gas masks and the large one that the baby will be put inside if there is a gas attack. It looks like a horrible big army-coloured egg with a funny clouded window and I am thankful that I am far too big to fit inside. I prefer my own red and blue 'Mickey Mouse' gas mask with its goggly eyes and whippy tongue although when I tried it on it was so tight it gave me a headache. There is our father's huge wireless, Hugh's big train set in its special box, several suitcases, the box of plants, the chests, the big trunk, several suitcases, the rusty old lawnmower, the mangle, Felicity's and Hugh's bikes and many crates and tea chests. Somehow the soldiers find room to fit in the all the last minute things.

"Come along, stop day dreaming and let me get you ready, dearest," Mother calls. She tidies my hair, re-ties my ribbons and checks to see that my socks are pulled up. She straightens the sash of my favourite sky-blue dress with the pattern of tiny white spots on it, which, she says, is made from pre-War Swiss lawn. Ted is neatly dressed in a frock belonging to Betty, my rag doll, because he doesn't have any boy clothes.

I stand on the front door step to watch one of the soldiers loading the animals; Clementina hisses and meows inside her cardboard prison and Poor Old Bunker, now tied by his lead to the handle of the summer trunk, looks very anxious as he tries to balance himself among all the baggage.

The other soldier helps Nan up into the cab, hands Lizzybuff up to her and then lifts me and Ted up. Mother climbs up last, helped by the driver, who is a short man with red hair. He asks her politely, "Everything in, is it, ma'am?" She climbs down and goes into the house for one last check.

I ask Nan if the new house is near Patisford. "Well, yes it is Henny, it's a little bit further south than this house at Burdock Coombe and it is closer to the sea."

"What's the sea?"

"The sea's the sea. That's what it is, the sea; just lots and lots of water with waves and boats sailing on it."

"Can we go to the sea tomorrow?"

"No, of course we can't. The Government won't let us.

8

One day, though, when the War is over, we will be allowed to go to the seaside and then you can play on the beach, build sand castles and paddle in the water. Ask your mother to tell you all about it when she is not too busy. She sailed on the sea in a very big ship when she went to Africa to join your father after they were married. Now just sit quietly." She rearranges us more comfortably beside her.

I whisper to Ted, "We're going to see the sea, to see the sea, to see the sea."

The Corporal helps Mother up into the cab once more. She turns to the soldiers in the back and tells them to keep a good eye on all our belongings and to make sure the animals do not fall out. As the lorry draws away from the curb Ted and I wave goodbye to Lloyd, the house, the garden and to everyone and everything that we can see. Mother waves grandly to our neighbours as they watch us leave. We sit down again, feeling very miserable that we are also leaving behind all the lovely coloured parachutes and the fat silver barrage balloons.

Ted and I start to doze off when an army jeep flying a red flag comes rushing down the road towards us. "Manoeuvres, ma'am," says the driver, "I'll have to back up until I find a lay-by." I sit up and want to ask him what 'manoovers' are, but he is too busy reversing the lorry. He eventually finds an entrance to a field; one of the soldiers opens the gate and the lorry pulls inside, well back from the passing vehicles.

Massive tank after massive tank rumble by and the dust eddies and swirls around us making us all cough. I hate the noise; it gives me a headache and makes me sneeze. Ted and I move even closer to Nan. Lizzybuff starts to whimper and then to cry. The animals hate what is happening too; Poor Old Bunker growls loudly, and wants to bark but Mother orders him to be quiet. Clementina is getting agitated and scratches the sides of her box, yowling and meowing non-stop. We wait and wait and it becomes hotter and hotter and noisier and noisier inside the lorry. It is almost like being in one of my nightmares. Then, finally, the last tank passes bearing a red flag, which, the Corporal explains to me, means the end of the convoy. Our lorry pulls back out of the field onto the road and we are on our way once more.

"We'll soon be out of all this military activity, Nan. Upper Nettlebourne is off the Plain, well away from the noise of constant tank fire, so it will be much quieter." Nan looks pleased and shifts Elizabeth, who has fallen fast asleep again, into her other arm. I wonder whether Hugh will miss playing in the burned-out plane on the wasteland across from our old house. He and his friend, William, played all sorts of games in it but would not let me join in and, because the plane was so high up off the ground, I couldn't climb up into it by myself.

"Are we nearly there?" I ask the driver.

"Another two miles, missy, and we'll be in your new village. Soon we will go over the bump," he adds. "It's what's called a humpbacked bridge and it goes over the bourne, that's a river to you and me! Here it comes, hold on tight!" The lorry goes over the bridge so fast that it seems as though we are flying through the air.

"Oh! Thank you! That was lovely. Are there any more bumps?" I ask him, my eyes shining with excitement. Before he can answer, Mother tells me to be quiet and orders the Corporal to go slower or else he will damage her valuable furniture. He apologizes and, when she turns away to look out of the window, he gives me big wink and I have to struggle not to laugh.

She looks across at us and says, brightly, "It will be a very pleasant house once we have settled in. I am glad that the Colonel arranged to have the whole house cleaned, the broken windows repaired and to have the inside walls whitewashed before we move in. The garden does need a bit of work, but, you'll see, it will all look lovely in no time at all."

"Broken windows?" queries Nan, sounding alarmed.

"It has been empty for many years, so I suppose some of them did get broken," she explains vaguely.

The lorry rattles down a steep hill and then, with joy in her voice, she exclaims, "There it is! There is The Old Manor Farmhouse - the lovely new home that your father and I chose for us. It is just waiting for us to move in and to live there happily ever after!"

Chapter 4
First Impressions

The house had once been painted white but the walls are now cracked and grey and partly covered with green leaves.

"That's Virginia creeper," Mother says. "In the autumn the leaves will change to wonderful shades of orange and red. We had that vine on my house when I was a child." She smiles at us happily and turns to the driver.

"Corporal, the entrance is on the village street side. There it is, on the left."

The lorry stops and the two soldiers jump off the back and try to open the big drive gates. "They won't budge, ma'am" one calls out cheerfully, "won't budge an inch."

"Push harder, young man," she shouts helpfully, "harder." They push as hard as they can but still nothing happens. "Would you mind giving them a hand, Corporal?" she asks. He gets down and all three of them put their weight against the gates. Still nothing happens so one of the men climbs over and shouts back that the long bolts have rusted shut. He struggles and eventually succeeds in loosening a bolt and they get the first gate open, which promptly falls off it hinges. This reveals, to Nan's and my total astonishment, a field of tall weeds.

"That's not a garden," she gasps, 'it's a Wilderness." She looks as though she is going to cry.

I am horrified, because I am sure that nannies don't ever cry.

I tuck my arm through hers and hug her to me.

"It'll take forever to clear all those weeds and bushes," she wails. "You are not strong enough with your bad back to do any of the heavy work, Mum, and I just can't do it all by myself, not even if Hugh and Felicity help me."

"Don't worry, Nan,' she replies calmly. "The Colonel has arranged for a new batman to help us six days a week. He will do all the heavy work in the garden and also in the house. He's away on a military exercise at present but will start work as soon as he returns."

"Will he be like Lloyd? Will he have pictures drawn on his arms? Will he let me ride on his back and hang on to his braces when he polishes the floors?" I enquire.

Ignoring my questions Nan tells my mother that she hopes the new batman will be a strong man. "He will need to be very strong indeed to cope with all this work." She shakes her head and suddenly looks very tired.

The second gate finally opens and the lorry bumps up what was once the driveway. The front door is at the back, which is odd. I notice that the roof is covered with moss; it does not look like a new house at all so now I can see why our mother calls it The Old Manor Farmhouse.

The Corporal helps us all out of the lorry and Mother takes a big key out of her handbag and unlocks the front door. I had seen this key in her desk drawer when I was looking for a pencil, but hadn't dared ask her what it was for because I am not allowed to open her desk. It looks more like a key to a castle, than a house.

We step inside. The house feels very old, very cold and very damp even though it is summer.

First the soldiers unload Poor Old Bunker, who disappears into the Wilderness and then Clementina, who dashes into the house and off upstairs. Mother shows the soldiers in which rooms to put the furniture and crates.

The first room we go into is the drawing room. We look out of the window at the semicircular front garden, which is also high with weeds. Mother tells us that there had been tall iron railings around it when she and our father had been to see the house, however, since then the Government had requisitioned them.

"What does "rekwishshishon" mean? Are you cross that they have taken them?" She explains to me that it means that the Government can take anything metal, even without asking, to melt down to build ships and tanks. She was happy for them to have the railings as long as we do not have to give up any more of our few remaining saucepans because, as it is, Nan is always complaining that, with a family our size, she should not have let the Government take so many. "However," she adds, "we have to do whatever we can towards the War Effort."

We can hear thumps and grunts in the background and what may be bad words, as the soldiers lug heavy furniture upstairs. The sun shines through the windows onto the paint-splashed dustsheets covering the floorboards. Nan moves one of the sheets aside and spreads out our old tartan rug on the floor and opens the picnic basket. She pours a cup of tea for our mother and one for herself from the Thermos flask and gives Lizzybuff and me beakers of milk. Ted and Lizzybuff sit beside me.

Finally, Nan reveals our treat, which are sandwiches made from real hard boiled eggs. The grocer sold us a dozen eggs as a favour because we were moving. "This was very kind of him," she remarks, "because, as we all know, the ration is only one egg each per week." Real eggs taste different from the delicious National Dried Egg that we usually eat and I don't think they are nearly as tasty.

"Nan, there's a problem with the dining room fireplace and there's also a large hole in the floor, so until we can get it fixed we will keep the door locked and have our meals in the kitchen."

"That will be easier in a way, won't it?" Nan replies. They continue to discuss this until I interrupt them with some very important questions.

"Where will I sleep?" I ask anxiously, "Can I have my

13

nightlight? Nan, did you bring Doggie and all my toys? Did we bring Lizzybuff's cot?"

Mother reassures me that they have remembered to bring everything and suggests that I stop asking so many questions and go and pick some flowers in the garden whilst they start the unpacking. She puts on my wellies and then opens the front door. We look out at the Wilderness, which looks scary and bewildering.

"I'll get lost!" I whine.

"Of course you won't, child," she says impatiently, "just don't go too far from the house and don't go near the river. The barns and stables are at the bottom of the garden and you can explore them another day with Hugo."

She closes the door and I push my way through the weeds, most of which are much taller than me. I try to stay close to the front door but soon lose my way. I pick a pink flower with fluffy bits that I haven't seen before, a few dandelions, some straggly poppies and a few small twigs with brown leaves.

Suddenly I hear a big, heavy, snuffley animal coming towards me through the undergrowth. It must be a lion. I am terrified. My heart jumps up and down inside my blue frock and I stand there, so frightened that I am unable to move, just waiting to be eaten alive. The weeds part and Poor Old Bunker appears. I am so relieved to see him instead of a ferocious lion that I give him a hug, which I have never done before. He smells disgusting and grunts and shrugs me off and continues to push his way through the vegetation towards the house. I follow him and then scuttle in front, quickly open the front door, rush inside and slam it in his face, leaving him outside. It serves him right for giving me such a bad fright.

I can hear the Grown-Ups talking and, clutching my flowers, I follow their voices down the long brick-floored hallway, through the dark scullery into the kitchen. They are busy taking pots and pans out of the tea chests and I help them as much as I can. Nan is still in her morning uniform, which is unusual. The old black range has been lit and I can smell a delicious cottage pie cooking in the oven. As another special moving day treat she says that I can stay up for supper. I decide to tell her privately about the lion when we are alone.

"What pretty flowers, sweetheart," Mother exclaims. "Are you all right? You look a bit flushed." I assure her that I am; I am not going to tell her about my fright, she might laugh at me. She unpacks the green vase and asks me to arrange the flowers in it and puts it on the supper table. She tells me that the name of the pink flower is willow herb.

The best thing about Mother is that she knows the names of all the flowers, all the trees, all the birds and all the animals in the whole wide world. She can also make all our clothes and toys as well as the special toys she makes to sell in London. She sews her own silk nightdresses, petticoats and camiknicks, whatever they are, and, when our shoes get too small, she knows how to cut the toes out, which makes them last until our cousins send us another lot of their hand-me-downs. But, very best of all, Mother can draw and paint and I am very excited about her telling me that she will soon give me what she calls art lessons.

Early in the evening the Big Ones arrive on the bus. Hugh gives one look at the Wilderness, says it's smashing and rushes off to explore. Felicity looks around and demands to know why we have moved to such an awful, tumbledown old place and whatever will her school friends think? Whilst Mother deals with her, I ask Nan if I can go and explore more of the garden with Hugh, but she says no, because it will soon be suppertime.

Hugh soon rushes back in, bursting with excitement about the barn and the stables and he tells us that he has already found a way inside through a broken door. He asks Mother if he can set up his trains in one of the lofts and hang his planes from the rafters.

"Yes," she agrees, "as long as you don't fall down the ladder and break your wrist like you did when we lived in Devon." That was when Hugo had a cast on his arm with a blue drawing of a giraffe on it, drawn, Mother told me, by the doctor.

Felicity explores upstairs and comes down saying that she quite likes her new bedroom and that it will be a good place for her to study. Just as she is closing the kitchen door, she stops, and tells us to be quiet. She stands there, listening. "I can hear footsteps upstairs," she exclaims, "and yet," she turns and looks at each of us, "we are all here. There must be a burglar in the house."

"Of course there isn't," Mother snaps, "these old floorboards creak and groan and make all sorts of noises."

Hugh interrupts, "I forgot to tell you, the air raid siren went when we were in the bus station. Everyone was rushing to the air raid shelter and then the All Clear went, so it must have been a false alarm. When it went off last term our form missed a whole arithmetic lesson sitting in the dungeon, which was wizard!"

Mother asks Nan if she knows where they have packed the blackout and the curtains.

"Oh dear," she replies, sounding very flustered, "I can't remember. Maybe they are packed in one of the suitcases, or in one of the tea chests? Shall I try and find them?"

"No, Nan, not now. It has been such a long and exciting day we shall all go to bed whilst it is still light and then we won't need to put them up until tomorrow."

"Please can I have my nightlight on?"

"Yes, dear child, you can. I don't think enemy aircraft will be able to see a light as tiny as that," she replies soothingly. Hugh sniggers quietly and, after checking to see that no one is watching, I stick my tongue out at him and he makes a very nasty face back.

After supper Mother says that she is too busy to come up to say goodnight to us so she kisses Lizzybuff and me and wishes us pleasant dreams. Nan carries the Little One upstairs and Ted and I follow. She leads us into our new night nursery and there is my small bed, Lizzybuff's cot and her bed. She has arranged all my stuffed animals on my bed with Doggie, my nightdress case on my pillow. I unzip him, pull out my nightdress and zip him up again. Ted and I never go to sleep without resting our heads on him. Nan puts on our nightdresses, tucks Lizzybuff up in her cot, helps me get under my bedclothes, says, "God bless you," as she always does and tells me that she will be coming to bed very soon. I whisper to her that I think it was a very good thing we that we didn't dig Pippa up and bring her with us and she smiles at me and nods her head in agreement.

She lights my nightlight even though it is not quite dark and quietly leaves the room. I like having the nightlight on, but I know, that, whichever house we are living in, once the room is dark the lamp will cast all sorts of scary shadows that grow bigger and smaller as the draught blows the flame.

Sometimes the room becomes so small I think that I will be squashed to death by the ceiling and sometimes it becomes so huge I can hardly see the ceiling. For all these problems it is still better than lying in the pitch dark without the lamp, not knowing what might be in the room waiting to pounce on me. I once overheard a grown-up say that bombs have names on them so when I hear the planes droning overhead night after night I lie awake shivering with fear and just waiting for the bomb with Henrietta written on it to be dropped on me and our house.

I often have terrible nightmares and cry out in my sleep. Whenever this happens, Nan climbs out of her bed, even in winter when it is so bitterly cold, shakes me awake and comforts me until I fall back to sleep. The very worse nightmare of all is the black and white one where I am being chased by a witch riding on a crocodile through a dark wood full of grabby things hanging from the trees.

Chapter 5
The Old Manor Farmhouse

The next morning I open my eyes and wonder where I am. I call out to Nan and she quietly explains that we are in our new night nursery. "Today we'll bring some of your toys and books up from the nursery and put them on the shelf by your bed and once we find the counterpanes and the curtains it'll look very nice."

"Can we put your pictures up too?"

"Yes, Henny, but I will have to ask Hugh to help us. We'll put the Lady in the Lily Field above my bed and maybe you would like to have the Lady holding the Baby above yours?"

"Yes, please."

She pulls down the sheet that she had put up over the window last night and sunlight floods the room. "I will go and dress and then get you up. We'll let Lizzybuff sleep for a few more minutes; you know how grumpy she is in the morning."

Ted and I lie on her bed and look around. The room is very large and the sunlight dances on the interesting pattern of cracks in the ceiling. There is a long window and a wide shelf runs the whole length of the front wall. There is a washbasin, our big wardrobe, a chair beside each bed and the table which has the nightlight on it. The soldiers have laid our old brown bedroom carpet on the floor and Nan's tin trunk sits beside her bed.

She returns and takes Ted and me along the landing to the bathroom, which is at the far end. She points out the linen cupboard and then opens the airing cupboard to show us its slatted shelves and the big boiler wrapped up in its padded coat to keep it warm. She closes the doors to keep the heat in and then I ask her to lift us up so that we can look out of what she calls the dormer window. I can see the Wilderness below and the barns beyond.

The landing floorboards squeak.

The bathroom is big and the lavatory is behind the door; it has a wooden seat and a long chain dangling from the tank. The bath has green marks inside it and funny animal feet with claws. The washbasin is too high for me to reach but Nan has put a

18

stool there for me to stand on. I am not sure I like the bathroom very much, it feels chilly and unfriendly and it is a long way away from the nursery downstairs. I hope that Nan will come upstairs

with me whenever I have to 'go'.

Back in the night nursery, Nanny wakes Lizzybuff while I tidy up my toys and then we go downstairs to the kitchen where Hugh is already waiting for his breakfast. We have fried bread and, as a special first day treat, cocoa, except for the Grown-Ups, who always have tea. Hugh says that he is in a big hurry because he wants to explore the barns further and have a better look at the lofts above. I ask him if Ted and I can go with him.

"No, Henny, you can't. I have to check it all out and then I'll let you come, but not that stupid teddy bear . . . "

"He has to first make sure that it is safe for you to explore the buildings," Nan explains hurriedly, "so let him go on his own and then he will tell us when you can go too." He smiles at her gratefully.

"That's right. I don't want you falling out of the loft do I?"

Why ever not, I wonder. He usually laughs when I fall and hurt myself.

"Hugh, once we've found the blackout, we have to put it up

at all the windows before dark. Otherwise, we'll get into trouble with Mr. Collins, the grocer, who is also the village Air Raid Warden. It's his job to check carefully to see that no lights show in the windows at night."

"Why, Nanny?"

"Oh! Please don't start so early in the morning. Why? Because the Government says so. It is just the same as it was at the old house; you know that, so stop asking silly questions."

"You may go in the garden now Hugh, but please come in and help me when I call you." Assuring Nan that he will, he hurries out of the back door.

Felicity arrives dressed in her best blue summer frock, which has a pattern of funny dark red and white circles on it and she is wearing her best sandals. "Why are you dressed like that?" Nan enquires.

"I thought I would catch the bus to town and look for a special history book I need for next term," she replies loftily.

"Oh no you don't, young lady! Go straight back upstairs and change into your work clothes. You are going to help us unpack all the boxes, all the tea chests, all the crates and put all the things away."

"You are not my Nanny, so you can't tell me what to do," Felicity retorts defiantly.

"Don't push my patience too far, Felicity. Maybe I will tell your mother how rude you have just been to me?" She looks ashamed and mutters that she is sorry and that of course she will help.

"When we have finished unpacking I want you to peel the potatoes for lunch please. Henny and I will wash up and then we can all get on with sorting everything out."

Lizzybuff sits in her highchair chatting away to herself in gobbledegook and watches us as we search through several crates, boxes and suitcases before we find the blackout and the curtains. Nan hands me the envelope of my drawings, which I put on the nursery table; she says that she will put some of them up on the toy cupboard door when she has time to make some flour and water paste. Felicity carries armful after armful of clothes upstairs and lays them on our beds to be put away later.

Then she takes her books out of the crates and carries load after load up to her bedroom. Trying to be helpful, I carry one of her really big books but trip on the last step and drop it. She shouts at me that I have broken the book's spine and that I have ruined her very best Angela Brazil Omnibus, whatever that is, and she will get even with me one day soon. I scramble back downstairs and stick close to Nan, hoping that she will soon forget that I have spoiled her book.

Later on Nan calls Hugh in and asks him to take his collections of daggers, coins and other interesting things up to his bedroom, together with the pictures our father sent him from Egypt before the War. These pictures are made of material and have strange flat faced people and flattened camels sewn on them. He tells us that he is going to hang his daggers on the sloping wall above his camp bed.

We stack my books and toys onto the trolley and push it over the uneven bricks of the hall floor and into the nursery. I put the books in the bookcase and Nan opens the toy cupboard in the wall beside the fireplace. A huge spider leaps out and Nan stamps on it before it can escape, poor thing. She brushes the shelves ready for the toys. I arrange some of them on the bottom shelf and she does the other ones.

The soldiers have placed the big wicker armchairs and the nursing chair near the fireplace. Nan pushes the big table up against the window so that I can sit at it to draw and watch what is happening outside. The tall brass-railed fireguard stands in front of the fire with the poker, shovel and coal scuttle inside it. Our old nursery carpet covers most of the floorboards.

Mother comes in and says, "Good morning, Nan, good morning, children. How is the unpacking going? I want you to help me in the drawing room but let's first have a cup of tea."

Chapter 6
The Grey Lady

It is time to unpack our special belongings in the drawing room. I settle Ted on the sofa where he can watch the goings on.

Our grandmother's elderly cousin, Janet, gave us two old wooden chests. The large one, known as Big Janet, is not just a regular old seaman's chest but is one that, according to my mother, had once belonged to a pirate named Captain Jack, who, with his faithful companion, the elegant Italian lady cat, Olivia, had had many adventures at sea. Mother stores her fur coat and all our winter clothes in Big Janet in the summer.

The summer trunk is the pale green canvas-covered steamer trunk, which our father bought at the Army & Navy Stores in London for my mother to stow her trousseau in when she sailed to Egypt to join him in the Sudan. There are several exciting-looking labels stuck on the outside, including one of camels standing beside some very strange shaped buildings. The smaller chest, named Little Janet, rests on top of the trunk. She is tied tightly shut so that all the sewing things cannot escape.

My mother stores her treasures from the past in the shallow

tray that fits in the top of the trunk; long evening gloves, exquisite bags and shoes, silk shawls and the ostrich feather fan wrapped in a piece of scarlet silk, and a book of old brown photos and a box of shiny black things she calls negatives. Under the tray we keep our summer clothes in winter, which is why it is called the summer trunk; it smells of the lavender bags that our grandmother made for her.

Beneath our clothes are Mother's evening gowns wrapped in layers of tissue paper. She knows how much I enjoy looking at them and so sometimes, on a wet afternoon, she takes them out and tells me about each garment and about the balls she had worn them to. There is a black one covered in sequins that shimmer in the light, a red silk shirt, a swirly long black satin skirt and the blouse she wore with it, which has a pattern made up of all the colours of the rainbow mixed together. That is my favourite outfit and hers too, although she said that our father prefers her to wear red. There is also an emerald green silk gown with pearl buttons, a long purple skirt, more silk shawls, a Japanese umbrella made from oiled paper and a long black cloak lined with slippery blue satin.

A valuable painted Chinese fan lies in a bed of silk in a black lacquered box decorated with magnificent gold patterns. On the fan there are mountains and a river winding through flower-filled gardens. The face of each person wandering through the landscape is painted on a small disc of ivory. I like to make up stories in my mind about the exquisitely costumed characters.

"Henrietta, stop day dreaming and put the silver calendar on the desk for me and then pick up all the newspaper." Leaving the exotic world of the fan, I obediently collect the scrunched up paper off the floor.

"We had better unpack the paintings next. They are in those special picture crates, Nan. We need the correct tool to open them, do you know where it is?" She says she can't remember. "No? Well then, I think that we should leave these until the batman can open them for us."

"What about Nanny's pictures for our bedroom?" I ask.

"No, Henrietta, I have just said that we will have to wait

for the batman's help. Let us deal with the china next." She takes wrapped parcels out of another tea chest, removes the paper and places the large platters and special dishes on the shelves either side of the fireplace. She places the precious china castle in the middle of an upper shelf where I can't reach it.

Next, comes the silver; I arrange pieces on the side tables and on top of her desk. She puts silver framed photos of herself, Granny and some other relatives on the mantelpiece. She takes out a large photo of our father in uniform looking very stern, presses it to her chest and murmurs something about her Beloved, kisses the glass and rests the photo in the place of honour in the centre of the mantelpiece.

With tears glistening in her eyes she asks, "Now where was I?" She pauses, "Let us see to the rugs next. Nan, can you untie the cords for me please?" They unroll the Persian rugs that our father had brought back with him after the First World War. My mother once told me the story of how he had helped rescue some of the Shah's many wives in an ambulance. I love the strange patterns and rich colours of these rugs and often think of the mysterious royal ladies and their brave escape.

"The house is already beginning to feel much more like home, isn't it, Nan? I think that we have already done enough for today. I feel tired and you must be too. Let us go and have our elevenses and then I will rest for a while on my bed. After lunch we will go for a walk in the village and introduce ourselves to our neighbours."

I sit up at the kitchen table and am busy colouring my drawing of the china castle. Nan has gone upstairs to take her special ornaments out of her tin trunk and arrange them on her bedside table.

Hugh comes in from the garden and says that he has something important to tell me. "I know something you don't know," he proclaims, tantalizingly, "and it's a very big secret. It's about this house."

"What is it? Tell me, please tell me, Hugh."

"No! You're too small to tell. You'll be so frightened that you'll scream the house down."

24

"No, I won't. Nan says I'm big now, what is it? Tell me."

"No! I can't tell you. You are only four so you are still a tiddler and far too babyish to be told grown-up stuff."

"Please tell me," I beg once more, jumping up and down in frustration. "I'll give you my biggest green marble, my bombsey."

"Give me *all* your marbles and I'll tell you."

I think about it for a few seconds and then agree.

"Well," he says, dramatically lowering his voice, "this new house of ours," he pauses, "is haunted."

I look at him blankly. "What is haunted?"

"It means that there is a ghost living here."

"What's a ghost?" I enquire, feeling very puzzled.

"You see, you are so stupid and so young that you don't even know what a ghost is." He scowls at me with a look of disgust.

"What is it?" I persist.

"It's, well, it's someone who is dead and they come back and walk around the house they used to live in."

"They're dead?"

"Well, you can't see them, stupid, but you can hear them moving about, you can hear their footsteps."

"In this house?"

"Yes. Mother says she's called the Grey Lady and she won't hurt us, but I bet she will. If you don't give me all the marbles, she'll EAT you!" he shouts, making scary faces at me.

I burst into tears.

"Oh! Stop it! *Cry baby bunting* . . . It just shows that you are far too young to know about this sort of secret. Anyway," he continues softly, "she lives upstairs and sleeps in the linen cupboard, but you will never see her, because she's invisible. Go up to your bedroom and get me all those marbles and then you'll be safe."

"I can't. You know we are not allowed upstairs in the daytime except to go the bathroom."

"Creep up. Go on, I'm waiting."

I climb the stairs as quietly as I can, scurry past the linen cupboard, go into the night nursery and collect my bag of marbles. Just as I am coming out of the room, my mother's door opens and, seeing me, she cries, "Whatever are you doing in your bedroom in the daytime?" Before I can even think of an answer, she slaps me.

I pelt downstairs, marbles in hand. There is no sign of Hugh. I rush into the nursery and, once more, burst into tears. "Whatever's the matter, Henny?" Nan asks, putting down the iron and bending over to hug me.

"Mother slapped me and Hugh says there's a dead lady living in the linen cupboard and if I don't give him all my marbles she'll eat me."

"Oh! Henny, you poor little girl! What nonsense! Of course she won't eat you. The village do say that this house has a ghost; your mother says her name is the Grey Lady. Although we may sometimes hear her footsteps on the landing, she won't give us any trouble and you'll never see her, so don't worry. You're quite safe. The reason your mother was cross was because you know that you are not allowed upstairs once the beds are made and the rooms tidied."

She hands me Ted and suggests that I tell him a story whilst she stacks some of the tinned food we brought with us on the cold marble shelves in the larder.

Chapter 7
Upper Nettlebourne

The main road from Patisford runs past one side of The Old Manor Farmhouse and the village street branches off past the other. The shops are further up on the other side of the main road.

My mother puts our ration books in her bag because she has to register them with Mr. Collins. We walk up the road to the grocery. She opens the door and we step into the sun-filled shop as Mr. Collins comes forward to greet us.

"Good morning, Mrs. Rowansforde, and how are you today? And who is this young lady?" he asks, bending over to shake my hand.

"This is Henrietta, my second daughter," she replies, handing him the ration books. He is short and plump and wears a spotless white apron looped onto one of his waistcoat buttons. The apron strings go around his waist and are tied in a bow on his tummy and when he comes out from behind the counter I can see that the apron almost reaches to the ground.

There is a shiny weighing scale on the counter and there are a few boxes and tins of food on the shelves behind the counter but most of the shelves are empty. By the window, which has gold letters on it, a large black cat rests sleepily on the top of a big barrel. There is an open sack of potatoes on the floor beside the barrel.

"On behalf of myself and my family and the rest of the village I would like to formally welcome you and Miss Henrietta, and the rest of your family, and your Nanny too, of course, to Upper Nettlebourne. I trust that you will be very happy here and if you need any help at all, please ask me and I will see what I can do. The Parish Council is very pleased to see a family moving into The Old Manor Farmhouse because it has been empty for far too many years. Nobody wanted to live there, you know, what with that great big garden to look after, and," he pauses and lowers his voice, "of course with the ..." Before he can continue my mother interrupts, a bit rudely, I thought.

"Yes, Mr. Collins, I quite understand," she says in her best no nonsense voice, "but little pitchers have big ears."

Maybe he was going to tell her about the Grey Lady?

He introduces his wife who smiles at us as she places a bag of sugar on the counter saying, "No charge, ma'am, the sugar is a small present from us both."

Mother thanks her and buys a few groceries from their meagre supply and he clips coupons from the ration books. He tells us that because he is the Air Raid Warden he has the only telephone in the village, which she is welcome to use in the case of an Emergency. I want to ask him what sort of Emergencies but I know he won't tell me.

He probably means bombs and explosions and things.

Mother thanks him and says, "The Colonel has arranged for me to have a batman but he is not available yet. However, we need to start work on the garden; the Wilderness, as our dear Nanny calls it. Do you know of anyone who would be willing to come and start scything what used to be the lawn for us?"

"That used to be a tennis court," he reminisces, "many, many years ago. I will see what I can do, ma'am, but as you know, all the young men have gone off to War. There's Old Perkins, I could ask him. He is well over eighty and as deaf as a post, but he can still swing a scythe with the best of them."

We leave the grocery and go next door to the baker's shop, where we meet Miss Hopkins. My mother places her daily bread order and buys us a hot crusty loaf for our lunch.

"Terrible thing if they start rationing bread, ma'am. As it is the Government does not issue us with enough flour to make bread for a village this size. Don't quite know what we'll do. But I tell you what," she smiles, "come blackberry-time, I will let you have some extra stale bread if you want to make some summer puddings. Nothing nicer than a good summer pud, and all the better tasting if it's made with stale bread, that's what I say."

Mother thanks her and says, "I hear that you make excellent Cornish pasties, Miss Hopkins."

"Well, I don't make them myself," she replies huffily, "my brother Fred, is the baker and it's his job. If you want to place a weekly order for say, half a dozen pasties, I'll let him know. They will be ready to be picked up from the bakery at one o'clock every

Tuesday." My mother says that five pasties will be sufficient and that one of the children will collect them each week.

We have my favourite Spam sandwiches for lunch and just as I am heading for the nursery to tell Ted about the shops, I overhear Mother saying, "The woman at the baker's shop says that bread may soon be rationed. If it is, Nan, we will starve."

I scuttle off, horrified.

Whatever will we do?

What can I find other than food to eat? Later that day I creep into the drawing room and carefully search through my mother's desk drawers. I nibble at the edges of a gum eraser, which tastes all right if I crunch it up really well, but it is not very filling and it is also rather dirty. I take out one of the black shiny things, which I know has something to do with photos, and try chewing it. It is quite tasty and will last a long time, because it is too hard to actually eat. I hide the eraser and several of the black things in the pocket of my green frock and ask Nan if I can go and play in the barn. She says I can and I hide my extra 'food' behind the manger where only I will ever find it. I now feel better because, even if we are starving, I will have a little something put away.

Mother asks Felicity and Hugh if they want to come for a walk with us to explore the village but they both say they are busy. We pass the cottage of our next door neighbour, Miss Jamieson, a retired school teacher. However she is out, so we will meet her another day.

Banks of cow parsley, dandelions and stinging nettles grow profusely on either side of a wide, deep, grass-filled ditch that runs along beside the street. Mother tells me, to my surprise, that this is the river. "Yes," she continues, before I can ask her why it has no water in it, "most rivers do have water in them. However, this one is a bourne – a winter bourne – therefore it is dry in the summer and fills up in the winter and spring. In fact, I hear that sometimes in December the water is so high that it overflows."

"How does the bourne know when it is time to fill up?"

"I don't know child," she replies uncertainly.

"What happens to the fish in the summer? Do they die?"

"Oh! Henrietta, for goodness sake! Stop asking questions, look where you are going and don't trip over your feet."

I bet they die, poor things; that's not nice at all.

As we come to the butcher's shop on the other side of the road, Mother says that she will go and meet the butcher tomorrow and register the ration books. There are dead wild rabbits hanging in the window with blood dripping out of their mouths. I stop to be sorry for them but Nan takes my hand, squeezes it and smiles down at me and hurries us on until we pass the Dairy Farm, where my mother has already placed an order with Mr. Blake for a churn of milk to be delivered every morning.

We continue on past the Village Hall and the inn, and then cross the bridge to the Church. Tall trees stand to attention on either side of the gate. Their gnarled roots stick out above the ground and I try not to step on them because it seems bad mannered, like treading on people's toes. There, through the thick leafiness of the trees is the Church set back from the gate in an untidy graveyard full of mossy headstones. Lizzybuff is fast asleep so Nan leaves her in the pram outside the church.

Mother pushes open the heavy, creaky, nail-studded door. Inside it is deliciously cool and peaceful and very small, especially compared to Patisford Abbey, which is very, very big, but it has to be big like that because it is God's house. The sun shines through the stained-glass windows, making puddles of colours on the old, worn flagstones. Nan goes out to see to Lizzybuff and we kneel and say our prayers and then, closing the door behind us, we join them in the churchyard. I quickly pick a bunch of daisies along the mossy path.

Leaving the churchyard, we soon come to the blacksmith's

forge where Nan lifts me up so I can see over the stable door. A red-faced man wearing a big leather apron looks up from the anvil and raises his hand in greeting. In the gloomy interior of the smithy I notice a young man pumping something up and down beside the chimney. Each time he pushes the handle down, the fire in the hearth flares up; with each upward movement it dies down. The blacksmith is hammering a length of glowing hot metal so hard that sparks fly off it and then he plunges it into a tank of water, it hisses in protest and clouds of steam erupt. He finishes what he is doing, takes off his leather gloves and comes over to the door and introduces himself as Mr. Watson.

"Well, well," he says smiling broadly at us all, "you must be the fine new family who have just moved into The Old Manor Farmhouse. It's good to see it being lived in after all these years."

Mother introduces herself and Nanny and tells Mr. Watson that my name is Henrietta and the Little One is called Elizabeth. "My eldest daughter, Felicity and my son, Hugo are at school in Patisford."

"Why don't you let your son come on Saturday morning to watch me shoe Violet and Clopper, the shire horses that belong to Mr. Blake at the Dairy Farm? Great brutes they are, but gentle as lambs really. I sing hymns to them whilst I shoe them and they give me no trouble at all. They like *Rock of Ages* best," he adds, smiling broadly at us. The forge smells hot and exciting. She says that she will see about letting Hugo come.

Mr. Watson informs her that his friend, Ned Green, is the village taxi driver. "With petrol so short, he seldom goes out, but if ever you have an Emergency, ma'am, and you need to go over to the doctor at Middle Brimsley, I'm sure he could find a gallon or two. He lives in the house just past the Post Office." She thanks him, and as we leave, he waves and smiles at me and I wave back, longing to tell Hugh about the forge.

At the end of the village street, we turn into a lane full of puddles that runs between two wide hedgerows and we decide to name it Watery Lane. We pick some flowers and then we come to a patch of big white daisies, which my mother says are called marguerites. She adds a few to her bunch together with some fern, takes a piece of wool out of her pocket and ties them up.

She says that we will go up to the woods in the spring and pick primroses and send Granny a shoebox-full in the post.

We come to a large log in the shade of the hedge and she says to Nan, "Let's sit here and rest for a few minutes. Just listen to the birds. When we go up on the Downs we'll hear the larks singing. Maybe this is a good time to tell Henrietta about the Grey Lady, Nan."

"She already knows about her," Nan says. "Her big brother told her all about the house being haunted and he really frightened the poor child, even telling her that the Grey Lady would eat her."

"Oh! Dear! He really is a menace!"

She calls me and asks me if I would like her to tell me a story whilst Nan takes Elizabeth for a walk up the lane. I sit quietly beside her and make a daisy chain, anxiously waiting to hear the next part of the tale.

"The new gown was finished, the carriage arranged, and I was waiting impatiently for the day of the Ball to arrive. That evening, my Nanny helped me dress and arranged my hair and then put my cloak around my shoulders, over my gown. My father and I climbed into the carriage and we were driven up the steep hill to the Castle. The full moon shone on the sea below.

"He escorted me into the Castle and to the receiving line where the Colonel and his wife were busy greeting each guest in turn. After they had greeted us, he slipped away and I walked into the very large ballroom, which was brightly lit by many chandeliers. The officers were all dressed in their finest uniforms for this splendid occasion. The ladies were dressed in their fashionable ball gowns, but I felt that mine was quite the most stylish and becoming. I joined a group of my friends. My dance card was filling up fast and I danced with several young officers whom I already knew.

"And then," she pauses, "a tall, dark, handsome young officer, whom I had never met before, approached me. He introduced himself and politely asked me for a dance. Number seven was the only one still free on my dance card so he wrote his name against it.

"When the seventh dance came it was a waltz," my mother

continues "the orchestra played The Blue Danube, and we waltzed and waltzed and waltzed. He was such a wonderful dancer." She smiles dreamily. "It was a very romantic evening," she pauses, and adds earnestly, "I really do think it was during that very first waltz that I fell in love with him. The Ball ended and I had to say goodbye to my new admirer, Captain Henry Rowansforde. He escorted me to my carriage, which had returned to take me home from the Castle. I was sad that the evening had ended so quickly.

"The next day, the Captain called at our house and left his visiting card. The following day he called again and asked my father's permission to take me to a dinner dance that evening at the finest hotel in the town.

My father agreed, and that was the beginning of a wonderful whirlwind month of tennis matches, tea dances, dinner dances, and dining with friends. We went for long drives in the countryside in a coupé, belonging to one of his brother officers. It was such a romantic time and each day I fell more and more in love with the handsome Captain."

She stops and gazes into space, remembering those happy days and looks as though she might cry and then she shakes herself, stands up and we continue our walk.

I run ahead and then stop because there, to my amazement, are several tiny, blue butterflies hovering over a muddy puddle. "What ever are they doing?" I ask. She says that they are drinking; I am astonished that such elegant creatures would drink such dirty water. She had told me that butterflies drink nectar, whatever that is, but it certainly sounds better than muddy water. "What are they called? Look! They have silver on their wings…"

"Chalk Hill Blues, Henrietta" Mother says, pointing to the Downs above the lane, "you can see why they live here with all those big mounds of chalk. I understand that our house is built of chalk and flint and that

horsehair was used to bind the materials together. One day soon we will explore the Downs and we will see lots more butterflies."

I finish the walk treasuring the colours of the butterflies in my head and decide to draw them when I get home.

Chapter 8
Briggs, the Batman

The Wilderness is still a great worry to my mother, however, because it is the summer holidays, both Felicity and Hugh join in and work hard. Felicity suggests that if she and Hugh clear all the old tin cans and other rubbish out of the front garden, Mother could ask the old man to scythe that too.

Old Perkins, who is indeed very aged and bent and dressed in ragged overalls, arrives one day and scythes the tall grass and weeds for us. He manages to cut the whole lawn area in just one day, working silently from dawn to dusk. He returns the next day and quickly tames the front garden. He accepts his pay, grunts, tips his cap and leaves as silently as he had appeared.

"The girls need something to wear when they are gardening Nan. We don't have any spare clothing coupons, so maybe I can make them some dungarees. Please see if you can find any suitable material in the summer trunk."

Nan searches and finds a length of green cloth. She lifts the sewing machine up onto the nursery table and whilst Mother cuts out the garments she tells Nan that she has to go up to London to see the buyer at Crosby's, the toy store, to obtain her Christmas order from them so that they can start planning and finding the materials to make the toys.

"But, Mum," says Nan sounding very alarmed, "It's only July. Couldn't you wait a bit longer until we are all settled in?"

"I won't go until Briggs is here and both Felicity and Hugo will be on holiday so I know you will manage well. I will only be away for two nights."

"Are you going to meet...?"

"I hope so, Nan, so be happy for me and I will soon be safely back home again."

Nan, who still looks rather worried, turns the handle and my mother stitches the dungarees up in no time at all. She makes one pair for Felicity, one for me and a tiny pair for Lizzybuff and tells us that they are our special gardening uniforms. I am very pleased because I have never been allowed to wear anything that looks like trousers before. I ask her if she can make Ted a pair out of the scraps and she says that she will one day.

"It's lucky, Nan, that the cousins sent us that pair of dungarees for Hugo and as they are a bit big they should last for a while. If he wears them when he's outside it will save his other clothes from getting ruined. You know what a mess he gets into."

We spend the long summer evenings weeding, tidying and raking the cuttings into piles. Hugh loads them into the wheelbarrow and empties it behind the barn. Nan and I weed  the brick path to the front door and the beds either side of it while Hugh attacks the saplings and small tree with a hatchet and a hand saw. Felicity decides where I should have my little garden, digs it over for me and then she and I plant my evening primrose roots. I feel very grown-up working with her. She tells me that she will plant the bulbs we brought from the old house in the autumn.

Briggs, the new batman, arrives early on Monday morning and apologizes for not being on duty at the house to greet us when we arrived. Mother tells him that she quite understands and that it is fortunate that he is here now. He is very tall and has twinkling blue eyes, wavy black hair and is in uniform.

She takes him into the kitchen and introduces him to Nanny and me and tells him that she has three other children; Felicity, Hugo and the Little One, Elizabeth, who is asleep in the nursery. She asks him about his family and he replies that he and his wife have three children, two boys and a little girl who looks about my age and whose name is Janey. They live in a quarter at the back of the nearby barracks. He plans to bicycle to work and back every day except Sunday, which is his day off.

"This is Ted." I hold him up for Briggs to see. "Our dog is called Poor Old Bunker because he is so miserable and our little lady cat is called Clementina," I tell him. He smiles and says he has a dog and a cat too. "What are their . . . ?"

35

"Be quiet, Henrietta. I am talking."

She informs Briggs of his duties; that he will be required to do all the heavy work in the garden, as well as the more strenuous work in the house, such as polishing the floors. "With the help of Old Perkins we have made a start on taming what Nanny still refers to as the Wilderness but there still remains a great deal to do. Felicity plans to plant and tend the old vegetable garden to keep us in produce throughout the winter once you have prepared the ground for her. Later on, the Parish Council expect us to Dig for Victory by also working an allotment. However, after seeing the state of the garden when we moved in, the Chairman of the Council has given us a grace period of a few months because the garden has been neglected for so long."

"We'll soon get it all shipshape, ma'am," Briggs says cheerfully, "I'm not afraid of hard work and you can depend on me to do my very best, both in the house and in the garden."

Mother tells him that the Colonel has suggested in one of his letters from overseas that, once he has settled in, we should think about starting to breed rabbits to sell in Patisford Market. His eyes light up. "I've kept rabbits since I was a young boy, ma'am. It will be a pleasure, a real pleasure. And," he adds, "unless the Colonel has informed you of a good place to get them, I have a farmer friend who breeds very good stock and I am sure that he would sell you a few to start with." By this time I am jumping up and down with excitement at the idea, which I had not heard a word about before.

"Please can I help you with the rabbits, Mr. Briggs? Can I help you look after them, please?" I urge.

"You just call me Briggs, young lady, and I will call you Henrietta, if that is alright with you ma'am?" he asks my mother. After slight hesitation, she nods in agreement.

"Please can we get the rabbits today?"

"Don't be so impatient," she replies with a laugh, "it's still only an idea at the moment. There is a lot of work to be done before we have everything ready to actually buy some rabbits. Cages have to be built and a place found to put them, however, I am sure that Briggs will be pleased to have your help." She turns to him and explains that I like animals very much, and, in fact, seem to prefer them to my brother and sisters. I don't tell him that my mother doesn't like animals and that Nan thinks that they have germs, because neither of them will be helping with the rabbits.

"She gets her love of animals from the Colonel. He went to Canada as a young man and was working on a ranch in the foothills of the Rockies when the First World War broke out. He left the ranch and joined a Canadian regiment and returned with them to serve his country. For various reasons he later joined the British regiment that he now serves with. If he had remained in Canada, a country which he loved very much, he told me that he would have trained to be a veterinary surgeon."

"Tell him about our grandfather galloping across the Plain in a horse drawn ambulance when our father got ill…"

"Be quiet! I am talking."

She leads Briggs out into the washing yard and delicately points to a door which, she informs him, is the outside lavatory and this is where he can change and leave his clothes. "You will need to give it a good clean first," she remarks, "It may be a bit dusty and cobwebby."

"I'll see to that first thing, ma'am", Briggs replies. He opens the door and looks inside and says that it will only take an hour or so to get the place spotless.

"Do what you have to do, Briggs, and then when you are ready, Henrietta will show you the sheds in the yard and later Hugo will show you the barn, the stables, the lofts and other parts of the garden that even I have not seen yet. It is such a big property to look after," she sighs, looking dramatically fatigued all of a sudden.

"Now," she beckons to me, "come back inside the house and help me clean the silver until Briggs is ready."

"Please can you tell me more of the story while we work?" She asks Nanny to make her a cup of tea and then agrees to finish the story that she had started a few days before.

"Now, where did I get to last time?" she asks me, gazing at her reflection in the newly polished Georgian teapot.

"The Captain had something to tell …." I remind her. "Oh, yes, I remember. Sit still, Henrietta, and don't fidget." I put on a suitably settled down look while I polish all the christening mugs. In her best story telling voice she continues the enchanting tale.

"Ten days after I had met him the Captain said that he had something to tell me. I was very excited! I thought I knew exactly what it was that he wanted to say but actually it was not at all what I expected," she pauses again and sighs deeply, "or wanted to hear. What he told me was that, at the end of the month, he would be posted for the next five years to the middle of the African desert thousands and thousands of miles away from my home," she sighs again looking downcast, as though she has just that minute heard the news.

"The remaining days flew by and we enjoyed every moment together. Then, the night before he was leaving, he went into my Father's study, closing the door behind him.

"After we had dinner with the family, the Captain and I walked through the conservatory and out into the rose garden, where we stood and watched the full moon shining on the sea and," she pauses, smiling at the memory, "he took my hand, and led me to the garden bench where we sat down. He told me that he had asked my father for my hand in marriage and that he had happily given his permission. He went down on one knee and proposed to me and I accepted, of course, and he took a small leather box out of his pocket which he handed to me and when I opened it, there, in a bed of dark blue velvet, was this exquisite diamond ring," she holds up her hand to display the ring, as she always does at this point in the tale. "As we had just become engaged to be married, I allowed him to kiss me for the very first time.

"My fiancé told me that although he was being posted to the Sudan for five years he would be given leave to return for our wedding and honeymoon and that I would be able to join him there some time in the future. The very next day he sailed away on a ship to Africa leaving me behind in England."

I beg her for more of the story but she does not seem to want to continue. She pours herself another cup of tea from the old brown teapot and paces around the kitchen restlessly. Finally, she sits down again, sighs deeply and gives the large, engraved tea tray an extra hard polish.

"Please tell me what happened next."

However, just at that moment, Briggs comes into the kitchen. "I now have that place cleaned out completely so all is well, ma'am. That is a lot of silver you have to clean, maybe I could help you with it sometime?"

Shaking her head, as if to bring her mind back to the present time, she laughs. "You are going to be far too busy, young man, to have time for cleaning silver. Now, Henrietta, thank you for helping me, you are getting quite good at the final polishing. Why don't you run along and show Briggs the sheds?" I breathe hard on the side of the tankard I am cleaning and give it an extra polish with the orange duster to show Briggs just how good I really am.

"Yes, I can see what you mean, ma'am. She is very professional," he smiles at me with a twinkle in his eye.

"The sheds are quite dirty, Briggs, so she must wear her old shoes, perhaps you will change them for her?"

I thank her for the story and give her a hug to cheer her up.

Once my shoelaces are tied I lead Briggs out through the back door into the washing yard.

"This shed is called the copper house and this tree outside it is called winter ...," I pause, thinking hard, "now what did my mother tell me? Winter something. The leaves are green now but she told me that as soon as it gets really cold and frosty they will turn bright orange and then red."

"Is it called winter heaven?" Briggs enquires gently.

"Yes, that's right, Briggs, winter heaven, of course that is the name, how silly of me to forget. I try and remember all the names she tells me because she gets a bit cross if I forget them, but you know," I look up at him, "she does tell me an awful lot of names. If I forget some, will you help me remember them?" He smilingly assures me that he will. "Winter heaven," I repeat again. "That's a lovely name isn't it Briggs?" Agreeing, he opens the door of the copper house.

"This is where Nan washes all the clothes; of course, she has to light the fire underneath the copper first. She doesn't like doing the washing in here at all because she says this place is dirty even though Hugh scrubbed the floor for her," I confide. "She has such a lot of washing, what with the Little One's nappies - Nanny's flags, that's what my mother calls them, and the sheets and all the other clothes too and Hugh gets his clothes so filthy and torn when he gets into fights." We go back into the yard and I show him the old mangle, the bed of mauve periwinkles and the long prop for the line.

Briggs, having had a good look around, says that perhaps he can do a few things to make the copper house more pleasant for her to work in. "She seems a very nice lady, your Nanny."

"Oh! She is not a lady, Briggs, she's a nanny. She and Ted are my best friends."

We go next door to the shed where we keep the coal and coke. "Hugh and I have seen lots of rats in here. He chases them with the coal shovel but he is not fast enough to kill any. I don't think that people should kill animals, but Nan says that rats bring germs and that they bite people. Is that true, Briggs?"

He agrees that it is and says that he will set some traps to get rid of them. "We don't want them getting into the larder and eating your supper now, do we?" I shake my head and laugh.

"This one is the tool shed, where we keep the tools and the wood. Hugh does most of the chopping and sometimes Felicity helps him saw logs but she doesn't like doing it at all. I wish I were big enough to use the saw and the axe, or even the little hatchet. Will you teach me, please?" Briggs agrees that he will when I am bigger.

"How much bigger?" I demand.

"Quite a lot bigger, young lady. What would Nanny say if I let you chop wood and you chopped your feet off by mistake?" I giggle and agree that she probably wouldn't be too pleased.

Hugh comes into the yard. "Hello, Briggs, I'm Hugo, but you can call me Hugh, like Henny does. I've been down at the forge watching Mr. Watson shoe a great big carthorse. Mother told me that I should show you the barns and the stables and the rest of the garden. You'd better ask Nan to put your wellies on, Henny; you don't want to get bitten by a snake, do you?"

Snakes? I think Hugh is fibbing but I'll ask Briggs later.

I rush back into the house and Nan puts my welly boots on and then I run across the freshly raked grass to the barn. In front of the barn doors is a large area of concrete where Felicity plans to practise her tennis shots against the doors. Briggs swings both doors open to let in enough light. The barn is very large with a high ceiling and at the back is a long, wooden trough built against the wall, which Hugh says is a manger where the horses would have been fed with the hay that used to be kept in the racks above it. Briggs asked Hugh what the inside room is.

"That's the Ghosty Hole," Hugh replies. "That is where some very nasty ghosts live, not from the same family as the Grey Lady who lives upstairs in our house at all; these are really bad ones," he adds, making hideous faces at me and growling fiercely. I grab Briggs' hand.

"Now, let me show you something." He reaches up to unlatch the Ghosty Hole door. I scream and run out of the barn into the sunshine. Briggs follows me and my brother comes behind quietly chanting, *"Cry baby bunting…"* taunting me under his breath. I take no notice, or pretend not to, whilst trying to stop shivering. Hugh tells Briggs that he will show him the inside of the Ghosty Hole another time when his scaredy baby sister isn't with them.

Briggs suggests that we explore the other stables and Hugh explains that each one had once been a bedroom for a horse and that the same manger and hayrack runs along the back wall. They are all empty except for some old boxes and some logs.

He leads us back into the barn and climbs up the ladder to the loft. The distance between the rungs is really big so Briggs climbs up onto the first rung and gently heaves me up with him all the way to the top. The only light in the loft comes in through a door, which Hugh has propped open. He says that in the olden days the farmer lowered the sacks of corn, which were stored in the loft, down onto horse-drawn carts in the farmyard below using pulleys and a crane, which are no longer there. He says that instead of a farmyard there is now a walled garden full of stinging nettles. I am much too frightened of falling out to go anywhere near that open door.

Hugh explains his plans for laying his train set out on the loft floor to Briggs, who agrees that it is an excellent idea and offers to help him hang his model planes from the rafters. He thanks him and says that having two people working on it will make it much easier. There are all sorts of interesting things in the loft; a pile of old sacks, a broken armchair, some deckchairs with torn canvas seats, a gramophone, a pile of dusty old records and a stack of badly torn magazines.

Safely on the ground once more, we walk around the back of the barn and look at the stinging nettles in the walled garden and then at the river, which is still dry. "That's why the village is called Nettlebourne, Briggs," Hugh explains. "Just look at all those nasty stingers!" We cross the riverbed into the cow parsley-filled wood. Walking in front of me, Briggs flattens the tall plants with his large feet, creating a path for me. Looking back across the river I spy a large white goat in the bottom of the next door garden but don't mention it to Hugh who is busy pointing out the tall elm trees where the guinea fowl from the Dairy Farm sleep at night. "They are the birds that make that funny ticking noise you hear as you go to sleep, Henny."

We return to the garden and inspect the big overgrown vegetable patch where we meet Poor Old Bunker walking despondently through the weeds. I introduce him to Briggs but he seems disinterested and wanders off. I show Briggs my own little garden and then we walk through the copse of fruit trees and show him the overturned stone drinking trough, which stands under an old cherry tree. Briggs tells us that it is called a thrush stone, and explains that thrushes fly to the stone carrying the snails that they catch and then smash their shells on it and eat the unfortunate inmates. The stone is surrounded by hundreds and hundreds of shattered bits of snail shell and they remind me of the tragic death of my dear little Pippa when I was younger.

Briggs sees that I am feeling sad and suggests that he gives me a piggyback ride back to the house. He kneels down, Hugh pushes me up onto his back and then Briggs takes off at a great speed, galloping around the lawn several times with my brother chasing along behind. We finally tear through the gate into the washing yard and arrive at the back door laughing hard.

I am very glad that he has come to our house and I feel much safer, because, if Briggs is now the Man of the Family, then Hugh can't boss me around any more.

Chapter 9
The Rabbits

At long last it is time to start building the hutches. Briggs collects the sawhorse and the tools from the shed. We go down to the barn and he opens the huge doors and brings out an armful of old planks that he has been collecting from all over the property and stacks them beside the sawhorse.

"Righty-ho! We'll make the first one six feet long and then put in two partitions and that will make three nesting boxes." He unclips his measuring tape from his belt and measures and marks several pieces of wood with a pencil.

I have dressed Ted in his dungarees and I perch him on a pile of logs where he can watch us. Briggs lifts me up and sits

me on the plank he is going to saw saying that my weight will help keep it steady. When he's finished he lifts me down and takes the planks into the barn. I run inside and watch him nailing the pieces together. He then says that we need some chicken wire for the sides and for the cage doors and wonders where we can get some.

"I know! I know!" I cry excitedly, "Hugh and I saw a whole roll of it all tangled up in the weeds in the walled garden. I'll show you where it is."

"I think you had better go up to the house and put your wellies on so that your legs don't get stung," he suggests. "Meanwhile, I'll fetch the sickle and the bill hook from the shed, and some heavy gloves - if I can find a pair," he adds.

"Are you having fun?" Nan asks. "Are you being a big help?" I assure her that I am and, thanking her for putting my boots on, rush out of the house to join Briggs as fast as my wellies, which are a bit big for me, let me.

Briggs fights his way through the tall weeds whilst I watch. There, almost hidden against the back wall is the roll of wire. He hacks at the weeds and nettles and then, using the gloves, he tugs and pulls the wire until it comes free. "This is perfect," he says, "it is very lucky that you and Hugh knew where to find it. All I need is a pair of wire cutters to cut it with. I couldn't find any in the shed, but maybe Mr. Collins, will lend us some. I will go over to the shop later and ask him."

We go back to the workbench and he finishes putting the planks on the bottom and the sides of the cage and tells me that, before the rabbits arrive, we will put some clean straw in the bottom of each nest so that they will have soft bedding.

"How many cages do we need to make?" I ask.

"Well," Briggs replies, "another two will be enough for now. However, when they start having babies and they grow big, we will need to make several more. We'll put the cages in a row on top of the manger at the back of the barn beneath the hayrack. In fact, thinking about it, the hayrack will be a good place to store the straw for their hutches."

"Will they be afraid at night?" I ask him. "Sleeping so close to the Ghosty Hole?" I shudder; I am afraid of this dark little room built within the barn, which Hugh told Briggs had probably been the tack room where they kept the horses' saddles and bridles. I will never go inside because I don't want to meet the ghosts who live there.

"They won't worry about that and you know why?"

"Why?"

"Because all good rabbits sleep all night long!" he chuckles.

"What colour rabbits will we get? How many? When will they come?" I ask impatiently.

"I don't know yet and it will be whatever colour rabbits my farmer friend can spare. I hope that he will sell us five girl rabbits and one boy and they will soon have babies - lots and lots of babies - and in no time at all we will have hundreds."

"What will we feed them on because my mother never has any food to spare?"

"Don't you worry! They love cow parsley, and it grows free all along the river bank and in our wood. They will also eat dandelions, dead nettles, cabbage leaves and carrots, anything like that; apple peelings, old bits of fruit and they love a heel of stale bread every now and then. I'll leave a piece of loose wood in each cage for them to gnaw on and then, maybe, they won't nibble holes in the cages."

"What are the rabbits' names?"

"I think my friend is much too busy to give them names so it is up to you to think of some. Now, it must be your lunchtime, young lady. We have done well; you have been a very big help. I'll have a word with Nanny and ask her if you can work with me again this afternoon. I can't possibly put the wire on the cages by myself."

I return to the house feeling very grown up and important. I don't say anything to Nan about missing my walk because I know that Briggs will arrange it. She agrees to his plan, but when she tells my mother she says no, she has other plans for Briggs. She wants him to polish the floors whilst we are out on our walk and that we can work on the cage tomorrow morning instead.

After our walk I draw a picture of the new cages and then a whole row of rabbits. I show Nan and she thinks it's very nice and says that the rabbits look quite real but that I need to give each one whiskers.

That night as I lie in bed I list all the names I can think of: Penny, Patty, Heather, Amanda, Janet, Joan, John, Freddy, Patty, no, I've already said that one; Ann, Rose, James, Nancy, Joy, Ann... I fell asleep and dream that there are hundreds of baby rabbits eating every single daisy in the whole garden.

We work hard on the cages and they are soon finished. At breakfast one morning Nan tells me that Briggs has a big surprise for me. I manage to stop myself asking her what it is. Oh! How I hope that the surprise is that the rabbits have arrived!

He comes into the kitchen for his morning mug of tea and says, "Well, Henny - can I call you that, like Nanny does?" I nod happily. "It is time for us to be off because I have something to show you." Nan hands me Ted and we dance ahead of Briggs all the way to the barn and when he opens the doors I see the rabbits peering through the netting of the cage doors, waffling their noses and looking very excited to see me. I am so happy I want to cry. "Can I take one out and play with her on the lawn, Briggs?"

"No, Henny," he replies, "they are not tame enough and if it runs away Poor Old Bunker will catch it for his supper. We don't want that to happen, do we?"

Briggs asks me what names I have chosen. I decide that the big grey one is to be called Heather after one of our cousins and then, pointing at each one, I name them Penny, Susannah and Belinda. He says that the next one is a boy so I call him Billy. "Why don't this one's ears stand up like the others?" I ask. "Are they broken?" Briggs laughs and tells me that she is a special type of rabbit and her ears are just as the Good Lord made them.

"I'll call her Floppy Ears, then."

"How many rabbits do we have?" I ask him.

"Six. Can't you count? A big girl like you? Look, there are two in that cage, one, two, and then two in this cage, three, four and two in the last cage that makes six. Do you understand?"

"No, not really," I reply, "my mother says that she does not want me to learn to read or write until I have learned to draw and paint because I'm going to be a famous artist when I grow up. I think that means not learning to count too."

"Well I never!" Briggs looks puzzled and shakes his head. "However, I am sure that your mother knows best. Here's a dry empty sack, let's go down the street and pick some rabbit food.

Come on, hurry up, they all want their breakfasts."

As we collect lots of juicy cow parsley I tell him about the big white goat I've seen at the bottom of Miss Jamieson's garden. "Please can you ask her if I can go and pet him, Briggs?" He says he thinks it will be better if my mother asks her. We soon fill the sack and return to the barn; he carefully opens the cage doors and gives each rabbit a big bunch of greens.

He says that he needs to discuss the rabbit arrangements. "I'll show Hugh how to clean the hutches out, which he will have to do on Saturday mornings. As Felicity will be too busy with all her schoolwork and later on with tending the garden she will not be able to help."

"She says she's studying for her School Stiffycat," I inform him.

"Yes, you are right. It means that you will have to collect the rabbit food each day because I have so many other jobs to do. Do you think you can do that? I will show you exactly what to pick besides cow parsley."

"Oh! Briggs, yes I can. Fancy me looking after my own rabbits!" I am so excited and I feel very important but then, about to cry, I say, "Briggs, I can't!"

"Why ever not?"

"Because the sacks are as big as me and I can't reach up high enough to put the food in the cages."

"Don't you worry," he assures me, "I have found some small sacks that you can use and the greens are not heavy at all. You're getting such a big, strong girl that I am sure that you will manage. I will put the food into the cages for you every morning and again before I go home in the afternoons and Hugh can do it on Sundays."

"Oh! Thank you, Briggs!" Feeling very relieved I smile at the rabbits and then at him and skip all the way back to the house, planning to tell Nan all about my new fluffy friends. Just as I reach the house Briggs calls out to me that I have forgotten Ted. I rush back and find him lying upside down in the straw. I pick him up and hug him tightly because I don't want him to think that I love the rabbits more than him.

After tea Nan asks Mother if she would be kind enough to

put me to bed because she still has some ironing to do.

She agrees that she will but first she wants to give me an art lesson. We sit at the nursery table and she opens her old tin paint box. "Look at all the colours; there are many different ones, aren't there?"

"Yes, lots. What are their names?"

"This one is rose madder, this is yellow ochre; that one is cerulean blue, the darker blue is ultramarine. My favourite, is cadmium red, the colour of the pillar boxes. Which one do you like best?"

"I think I like," I hesitate, "the yellow one and that one," I tell her, pointing to a bluey-green paint.

"That one is called turquoise."

"Turk woz," I repeat. "What a lovely name."

"Now, you have to learn to mix your colours, Henrietta. Red and blue makes yellow, blue and yellow make green, red, blue and yellow make brown. All colours can be mixed from red, blue and yellow. Do you understand? I will teach you to mix the colours and, until you are twenty one years old, you will only use those three colours. White is never used in watercolour; if you want white you just leave the paper blank." She shows me how to mix the colours, to wash my brush after mixing each colour and how to make sure I don't get the paper too wet.

We go upstairs and my mother gets me ready for bed and then sits on the chair beside me and sings:

> *"Hush, here comes the sandman*
> *Hush here comes the sandman*
> *Now you children run up the stairs*
> *Put on your nightclothes and say your prayers*
> *Hush, here comes the sand..."*

Chapter 10
The Big Drama!

It is a hot, sunny morning and I have dressed Ted in the blue trousers that Nan has just knitted him. We are lying flat on the nursery table peering out over the windowsill checking for interesting snails in the flowerbed below. I wriggle out a bit further and spot several, along with a worm and a very big shiny black beetle scurrying along between the plants. I look up and see something very strange at the edge of the lawn.

"Look, Ted," I grab him excitedly and point to it. "Whatever do you think it is? Do you think it is a present for us? I wonder

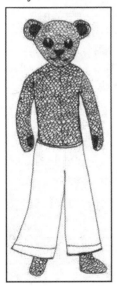

who sent it. Do you think our father did? It looks like a big pointy egg with funny things at the back. I know that Hugh will like it. I'll just climb down and have a better look. You stay there, and tell me if a Grown-Up comes."

I am still struggling to open the window further when Nan comes into the nursery.

"Whatever are you doing, Henny? Trying to climb out of the window? You know you are not allowed to do that. I certainly don't want you playing with these old sash windows because the cords could break at any moment and then the window will come crashing down on you and hurt you. Why did you want to go out in the garden?"

"Because there's something special on the road by the edge of the lawn Nan, and we think it might be a present for us and I wanted to climb out and have a look at it."

"What sort of something on the road by the edge of the lawn? Whatever do you mean? Is this more of your silliness, Henrietta? What is it that you can see?" she asks, glancing out of the window.

"There, Nan, that funny thing over there."

"Where?"

"Lean out more and then you'll see it."

She leans out and exclaims, "Oh! My goodness me! Come

away from the window at once. Run out into the garden and stay there. Mum," she shouts louder than I had ever heard her shout before, "get the children out of the house, quickly, there's a bomb!" I grab Ted and climb down off the table just as Mother rushes into the nursery. She leans out of the window, sees it and slamming the window shut, grabs me and Ted and we all rush out into the hallway.

"Nan, you put Elizabeth in the pram. Out you go into the garden, Henrietta, and wait for us there. I must wake Hugh and Felicity up." She yells loudly for them, and they both appear at the top of the stairs looking very sleepy.

"There's an unexploded bomb on the road by the front lawn. Hugo, come downstairs now and open the gate and help Nanny with the pram. Felicity, run down the street and warn our neighbours to leave their houses too."

Felicity replies, "I can't! I am in my nightdress; I'll have to change first."

"No! Put on your dressing gown and go. Now! This minute! This is an Emergency! Take everyone down the street Nan, as far as the church and wait there. I will go over to the shop to call the army."

"Oh, Mum, do be careful," says Nanny anxiously, "don't go too close to the bomb, it might blow up."

She replies that she will climb out of the kitchen window and take the long way around through the field. "I'll take great care, I'll be all right, don't worry. Now," she commands us with excitement ringing in her voice, "go as quickly as you can everyone."

Nan always says that my mother loves a good Drama.

We rush out of the gate and down the street with Nan pushing the pram as fast as she can.

"Look! There's Briggs on his bicycle, right down by Mrs. Babcock's shop," Hugh cries.

"Oh, thank goodness! Now run, Hugh and tell him what's happened and ask him to come and help us."

My brother tears down the street yelling to Briggs that there is an Emergency and when he reaches him he jumps up onto the

51

handlebars and Briggs pedals furiously to meet us. He leaps off his bike and, telling Hugh to hold it, he grabs hold of Ted and me, puts us up on the pram seat, takes the pram handle from Nan and pushes us at top speed down the street.

He orders Felicity to run ahead and knock hard on our next door neighbour's front door, which she does. The upstairs window flies open and Miss Jamieson leans out. "Whatever is happening?" she asks. Her long ginger hair is loose and all over the place. I wish my hair was that colour.

"Get out, lady, get out," shouts Briggs, "there is an unexploded bomb in front of our house, come with us to safety down by the church."

Miss Jamieson quickly reappears wearing a very shiny blue quilted dressing gown and her bedroom slippers. "What about the goat?" I ask her, anxiously. "Can I go and fetch him? I don't want him to get hurt."

Before she can answer, Briggs tells me that there's no time; the animal will be alright and I shouldn't worry. "Hugh, jump on my bicycle and go and warn all the neighbours all the way down as far as the church, you'll be quicker than Felicity on foot."

Hugh puts one leg under the bar and rides off quickly, wobbling a bit, but happy to have the chance to ride a man-sized bicycle. "Where's your mother?" Briggs asks anxiously.

"She's gone over to the shop to phone the army," Nan replies.

"That's good! They will soon be here. Come on everyone, let's see how fast I can push the pram, come on Nanny, and you too, lady, RUN!" he shouts at Miss Jamieson, with laughter in his voice. Lizzybuff claps her hands and chuckles with delight at all the excitement. Briggs quickly makes it seem as though we are having a good time. "Let's pretend we're running races at the village Fête. Come on, Nanny, faster!" We must be a very strange sight, tearing down the street in the early morning, laughing fit to burst.

We reach the church and the neighbours who have followed us all want to know more details about the bomb. Felicity informs them all about it, although she has not actually seen it.

The second she stops to draw breath, I call out, "I saw it first, didn't I Nanny? It is on the road by our front lawn, just outside the nursery window."

"Yes," she agrees, smiling shyly at the assembled group, "Henrietta did see it first and it was she who called me to have a look." She smiles down at me fondly and Felicity does not look too pleased. Nan suddenly realizes she is still wearing her grubby cooking apron, instead of her usual white one over her morning uniform. She blushes with embarrassment, hastily takes it off and hides it in the pram.

"My mother," Felicity proclaims loudly, trying to regain everyone's attention "has gone to telephone the army."

"That's good," says Miss Jamieson, who, by this time, to my dismay, has managed to get her hair into some sort of order. "I expect they will be here soon and will deal with it quite quickly. Why don't we play "I Spy", children, whilst we are waiting? I will begin. I spy," she pauses, "with my little eye, something beginning with C."

"Tree," shouts Hugh triumphantly, much to the amazement of the gathering, except for Lizzybuff, Ted and me because none of us have the faintest idea what letter anything begins with.

"C, Hugo, C not T," says Miss Jamieson, gently, "I think you misheard me." Hugh turns pink and looks away. Fortunately, at that very moment, he sees Mother climbing over the stile at the back of the churchyard.

"I spy," he cries loudly, "My mother! Look, she's coming into the churchyard through the back way. She has Poor Old Bunker with her too." He runs to meet her and then rushes back to ask Briggs to lift the dog over the stile because he is too fat to squeeze through.

"Did you bring Clementina?" I ask her.

"Of course not! Don't you worry about her, Henrietta; cats are well able to look after themselves."

"What about the rabbits? We could have put some of them in the pram..." She looks impatient and as though she might not like the idea of animals being mixed up with Lizzybuff so I smile at her brightly, tell her that I am very glad that she didn't get blown up and then promptly burst into tears.

"Nanny, please cope with her." She turns her attention away from my snivelling self to the ever-growing crowd. Using her best voice, she declaims: "I have telephoned the army and they are despatching a bomb disposal team from the camp at Pinchton Magna. All our neighbours, from the grocery shop up to the Post Office are perfectly safe; they have gone down the lane to the bakery." She turns to us, "Briggs, I am so glad that you were here to help Nanny and the children." She smiles at him and he gives her a funny little bow.

"Look," shouts Hugh, a while later, pointing back down the street, "there's the army, right outside our house. There's a big lorry and a jeep, I hope the soldiers don't get killed," he adds lugubriously, "that bomb could go off at any minute and blow our house up and kill the lot of them…."

"Stop it, Hugo, stop it at once," Mother orders sternly, as she sees how frightened I look and that I am about to cry again. "That is quite enough, they are the experts and they know precisely how to handle all sorts of bombs, and besides, I don't think that it is a very big one," she smiles reassuringly at the gathered crowd, as though she is an expert on bomb sizes.

We wait and wait and I am very worried about all the animals left at home but eventually a jeep drives down the street, stops at the Church and an officer jumps out. He salutes and says, "All clear now, ma'am. There is a crater where the bomb landed on the road at the top of the hill just outside the village. The bomb must have bounced and then rolled down the hill and come to a stop at the edge of your lawn. It is very fortunate that it did not go off when it landed, because even that far away it could have blown this whole village to kingdom come, you know! Might have wiped out the lot of you! It must have been dropped by an enemy aircraft emptying its bomb bay on its way back to base. Pretty poor show, you know! However, we have defused and removed the bomb so it is quite safe for you all to return home." He thanks my mother for alerting the military, salutes once more, jumps back into his jeep and speeds off.

"What an adventure!" Mother cries. "What an exciting start to a Friday morning! Come along children. Briggs, do you know where Hugo is?"

"Just trying out my bicycle, ma'am, he'll be back in a minute. Nanny, can I help you push the pram?" he asks with a twinkle in his eye.

"No, thank you, Briggs," she replies formally, "I can manage quite well now all the excitement is over." I notice that she gives him a shy smile.

We troop home and when we reach our garden there, waiting at the gate for us, is Clementina, who had not run away to safety at all. I give her a big hug and whisper that I am glad she has not been blown into a million furry pieces. She rubs against my legs and purrs and follows me into the house telling me that she is very hungry indeed and needs her breakfast.

Chapter 11
Over the Hills and Far Away

Felicity says that the best potatoes grow in the allotment behind the butcher's shop but that the large vegetable patch in our garden is better for growing all the other crops including strawberries. One sunny morning we go down the street to the allotment and after she has dug up the mother plants I find lots of large potatoes and a few small ones and we put them in our trugs; she has a big one and I have my own little one as well as my own small fork and trowel.

I feel very grown up as we march down the village street, my matching big sister and I in our new green dungarees and wellies carrying our trugs full of our home grown potatoes. I glance down the street towards the Church and see an old tramp in the distance. I ask Felicity to hurry up so that she can tell Mother that he is on his way so she will have time to pack up some food for him.

When the tramp reaches our garden I open the side gate and wish him good morning. He smiles at me, raises his battered felt hat and pushes his decrepit old pram up the path. Boxes, bags and parcels of books, in fact, what Mother later describes as 'all his worldly possessions' are fitted into or onto the pram, all securely tied with rope, odds and ends of wire and bits of string.

She is waiting for him at the front door. He raises his hat to her and smiles at us both. "Good morning," he greets us politely. "How are you and the family, ma'am? It is a blessing to be here with you because I have heard that this is one of the few families who welcome us travellers."

He has bright blue eyes, spectacles and a long white beard and although the weather is still warm he wears several layers of clothes under his black overcoat. Because all his coat buttons are missing he has tied his coat shut with an old piece of rope. My mother hands him a paper bag, in which, she told me later, she had put a small package of sandwiches, tea leaves in a twist of paper and a jam jar of orange juice made from our allowance.

She often reminds me that, however little food we have, we must always give to those whose needs are greater than ours. She never, ever turns anyone away empty-handed. She told me one day that no one knows when the Lord Jesus will return, or whom He will come back as, so, I suppose, that just in case the tramp is Jesus, she also gives him an old jersey and a very warm woolly scarf that Hugh had found in a hedge somewhere and which Nan has washed and mended and which now looks as good as new.

"Thank you, ma'am, that scarf will keep the wind out when the weather gets colder, and thank you for the very welcome parcel of food. Not many people share the little food they have these days, I can tell you." He shakes his head sadly.

"Where are you off to?" I ask.

"Over the hills and far away," he replies with a smile.

"Where to? Where to?"

"I'm going over the Downs to Patisford but these days I have to be careful to keep away from the firing ranges, so I watch out for the red flags, and try to keep out of trouble. "Then," he continues, "I always stop at the Abbey and go in to thank the Good Lord for keeping me safe for another year..."

"That's where the Good Lord lives, isn't it? It's His house, isn't it, Mother?"

"Yes," she agrees, smiling a grown-up smile at the old man, "that's right."

"That's right," he agrees, "that is very right indeed."

"And His house is even colder than our house."

The tramp chuckles and says that I am probably right about that too. My mother looks a bit put out by my remark.

"Come back soon," I call to him as he put the things in the pram and starts to push it down the path and then he stops and says that he has just remembered that he has something special to show me. There in the pram, fast asleep in a box lined with bits of sheep's wool, is a tiny tabby kitten curled up in a ball. He tells me that this is his new companion and that when the kitten grows up into a really big, strong cat he will teach it to catch fish and wild rabbits for their supper.

"What is the kitten's name?"

"He doesn't have one yet. You can choose a name for him."

"Wellington," I answer promptly, "My big sister told me

57

she learned about him in her history lesson and she said that he was big and strong and a brave fighter like our father. Our father is fighting for England, you know, and when the War is over, and there is World Peace, he'll come home and live with us here," I assure him, earnestly reciting the words that Mother keeps repeating to us children.

"Oh, I've heard that your father is a great man, missy, and I think Wellington is a grand name for a wee cat. I can always

 call him Welly for short, like our boots!" He chuckles, and then, looking very serious, he turns to my mother and asks, "I don't suppose, ma'am, that you could spare me a little meths for my poor blistered feet, could you?"

Her mood suddenly changes and she replies coldly that she does not have any methylated spirits and that it is time for us to go inside, and for him to leave.

The old man looks disappointed, but as though he understands. "Well then," he says, "I must be on my way, and God bless you, ma'am, and you missy, and all the family. We will see you next year, by which time," he beams at me, "Wellington will be a big grown-up cat!"

He leaves and I close the gate after him, having given the kitten a quick farewell stroke, and follow Mother into the house. I know that somehow his question about the meths had spoiled it all. I know that Nan uses meths to fill the Primus stove, which she then pumps and lights it if she wants to cook something on it. I know there is at least one big bottle up on the top shelf in the copper house.

However, I have learned to keep my mouth shut whenever Grown-Ups tell fibs.

Later on, I ask Nan why we couldn't have given him some meths. She replies that she had heard that putting it on sore feet helps to harden them, but that the tramp probably wanted it to drink. To drink it? Surely he would catch fire? What about

58

the kitten? Oh dear, it was all very worrying, like when grown ups smoke cigarettes. It seemed such a strange thing to do, to fill themselves up with smoke. After all, you never see animals smoking do you? Well…dragons do, in books, but then they are special and they breathe fire too, so they need to smoke. Even my mother smokes a cigarette before lunch on Saturdays with a glass of sherry, if she has any.

At teatime I tell Hugh about the kitten and how he is going to grow up to be big and strong enough to catch fish and wild rabbits for him and the old man to eat.

"Don't be so stupid," retorts my brother rudely, "the rabbits will kill him first."

"They won't, will they, Nan?"

"Or he'll jump out of the pram and get squashed by a lorry and be strawberry jam, all over the road, a big puddle of it and…" I burst into tears, "He won't will he, Nan? The old man won't let him jump out, will he?"

"No, of course he won't. Stop that, Hugh, stop it at once; be quiet and eat your supper. You know how much Henny loves animals and you really upset her when you tease her like that."

She turns to me with a smile and reminds Hugh that school is starting again next week. "Then we will have some peace and quiet, Henny, with just you, me, Lizzybuff and Ted."

Hugh looks very unhappy at the idea of the holidays ending. Nan tells him to go and feed the animals whilst we wash up the dishes. She suggests that we recite the *Three Little Kittens* poem together to cheer me up. I give a huge shuddering sigh, a hiccup or two and a big gulp, and let her blow my nose without wriggling and then we begin:

> *"Three little kittens, one stormy night,*
> *Began to quarrel and then to fight . . ."*

Chapter 12
Things that go Bump...

"Not far now, Henny," Nan says encouragingly, "we'll soon be at the shops. Come on, don't lag behind."

"Nan," Hugh says, "I want to go up that shortcut. It comes out opposite the chemist's shop."

"Take your sister with you, Hugh. You'd like that, wouldn't you?" she smiles at me, "and," she continues, "hold her hand..." However, when she sees the look of disgust on my brother's face she laughs and says, "Well, Hugh, I expect that she is big enough to manage on her own, but look after her and wait for me by the road because I need your help crossing what with all the military traffic. Now look where you're going and don't trip over your feet," she admonishes me with a loving smile.

I follow Hugh up a narrow path bordered on both sides by very tall grass and cow parsley. Hugh finds a hazelnut bush and we stop to pick some nuts. He picks those on the higher branches and I from the lower ones and put them in the pockets of my green frock. I'll give Nan some to put in the pram to take home and I'll add the rest of them to my secret store of 'food' in the barn. However, I will have to find a tin to put them in or the rats will eat them.

Hugh rushes ahead but I see a patch of poppies and I call out to him, "Hugh, look! Poppies! I'll pick some to take home."

"Well be quick and don't let them stain your frock."

I pick some that are open, some that are still half asleep and a few seed heads, which my mother really likes. "Hurry up, Henny, or Nan will be there first."

I look down and there at my feet is a tennis ball. However, when I pick it up I find that it is only half a ball. "Look what I have found, Hugh!" I proudly hold my prize aloft.

"That's not much good, Henny. Whatever can anyone do with half a ball? Play half a game?"

"Well, I like it. It's going to be a present for Briggs."

"He won't want it, stupid. Come on, hurry up." He takes off at a run and I stumble after him and then come to a sudden halt.

"Look, Hugh, it's a maderall, isn't it? Look at all the colours on its wings."

"Oh, come on," he repeats crossly, but comes back to see what I am talking about. "That's just a common old Red Admiral stupid, not a *maderall*," he imitates my voice. "Come on, stop keeping on stopping or I'll get really mad."

Wishing the butterfly a silent goodbye I follow him to the top of the path and Nan and Lizzybuff are waiting for us. I hold up my flowers to show her.

"What lovely poppies! Your mother will love them. And what is that in your other hand?" I hold up the half ball.

"It's a present for Briggs, Nan."

"I'm sure he'll be very pleased with it."

"Nan?"

"Yes, Henny, what is it?" I pull on her sleeve and go up on tiptoe to whisper in her ear. "Do you want to 'go'?" she asks rather crossly.

"No thank you, Nan."

"What do you want to tell me?"

"That is Fairyland," I confide, trying to make sure Hugh does not hear me, "right there. It really is Fairyland, you know."

"Yes, Henny, that's nice isn't it? Now, we have to do our shopping. Hugh, help me get the pram down off the pavement. Hold onto the handle, Henny. There's nothing coming; let's cross the road now."

Mother is pleased with the poppies and Briggs likes the half tennis ball and says he will take it home to show Janey. I tell him about Fairyland because I know he will not laugh at me and he agrees that every time I go up that path I am sure to find something special. He says it's time for him to go home and that he will see me in the morning.

I sit up at the kitchen table happily drawing a picture of the poppies and then colouring them as red as I possibly can. I try to draw the butterfly as well but it looks a bit wonky.

"How much longer can it go on, do you think, Nan? It must be at least an hour since the tank convoy started." The windowpanes rattle and the house shudders. "Just look how

61

dusty everything is. I never thought that we would have to put up with military manoeuvres this far off the Plain."

"I don't know, Mum, but I think that we should take our supper into the nursery, it is warm in there and it should be less noisy." She flinches as a particularly heavy-sounding tank passes, and adds, "and much safer."

Mother starts organizing us all. "Felicity, please help me load the supper onto the trolley; Hugo, you help me push it and try and stop the loose wheel coming off. Nan, can you wheel Elizabeth in, in her highchair? Yes, tip it back a bit and then push, I know the brick floor is uneven, but it is quicker than taking her out of the chair. Come on everyone, it'll be much better in there." We hurry out of the kitchen into the nursery and arrange our supper on the table.

"Hugo, help Nanny pull the table out from the window to make enough room for us all to sit down and then bring in some chairs from the kitchen."

Just as we have settled down to eat, there is a tremendous crash. The whole house shakes, Lizzybuff begins to cry and Poor Old Bunker barks frantically in the kitchen. The Grown-Ups leap to their feet but Hugh is already out of the door. He rushes back into the nursery shouting that a tank has hit the corner of the house. "Come quickly, there's a great big hole of the kitchen wall."

We all run out of the nursery leaving Lizzybuff strapped in the highchair, crying.

"Stay with her, Henny," Nan orders, but, because I don't want to miss the excitement or miss seeing the hole, I ignore her for once and follow the others into the kitchen.

"Great heavens above!" my mother gasps. "Look at it! Oh! Nan, whatever can we do?" she wails.

A few minutes later there is a knock at the front door. Hugh answers it and returns with an officer and a couple of soldiers. The officer introduces himself to my mother and apologizes profusely and assures us that the army will fix up the damage as good as new the next day.

"What about tonight, young man?" she demands crossly. "The autumn nights are becoming much colder, and my husband, the Colonel, would not expect his family to go to bed with a huge gaping hole in the kitchen wall."

The officer replies nervously that he will have some of his men patch it for us immediately if we have any spare sheets of corrugated iron or planks that they can use.

"Hugo, take the officer and his men down to the barn. Take the big torch but don't switch it on until you are inside the barn with the door closed. See what materials you can find to fix this problem for tonight." Looking very important and pleased with himself, he takes them out into the pitch dark garden.

Eventually, the soldiers manage to close the hole to Mother's satisfaction and return to their tank. Nan suggests that we leave the range burning all night to combat the cold air seeping through the cracks in the walls. The officer takes his leave after first assuring my mother that he will send a team the next morning.

"And I thought living here would be much quieter once we had moved off the Plain. How wrong I was!" she remarks.

"At least no-one was hurt, Mum," Nan replies, "not even the tank! Let's go back and finish our supper. Oh! My goodness! I forgot all about Elizabeth, the poor little darling."

We hurry back into the nursery and there is our dear little Dormouse fast asleep in her highchair with her face in her dish of cereal. Nan gently unstraps her and lifts her out of the chair. She never even stirs when Nan carries her upstairs to wash her and put her to bed.

I ask Mother if she will come upstairs and tell me a quick story and she agrees. She sits beside my bed and is about to begin when I beg her to tell me about the wedding.

"No, Henrietta that comes later and, with your father still away, it makes me sad to remember those happy days but I will tell you another part of my story if you sit down and listen quietly."

"I wrote to my fiancé very often and I received many letters back from him."

"You didn't start the right way," I say, beginning to chant, "Once upon a time…"

"One night," she continues, looking at me tiredly, "I dreamed that he was sitting up in bed in his tent in the desert with his leg in a plaster cast. I wrote a letter and told him about my dream and a week later I received a letter from him saying that he was writing to me sitting up in bed in his tent in the desert with his leg in a plaster cast. He said that he had fallen off his pony during a polo game. Our letters had crossed in the mail." She had explained to me once before what that meant.

"A year and a half after my fiancé went to Africa my mother, your grandmother, started planning my wedding. A week after my fiancé returned we were married, but that," she says with a happy smile, "is another story."

"That was our father who you married, wasn't it? Will he be coming to see us soon?" I asked.

"No," she replied, "he is . . . "

"Thousands and thousands of miles away...." I parrot remembering the words of the earlier part of the story.

Looking very dismayed she mutters: "Yes, that's right, all these years later, and once more, he is, as you so kindly remind me, Henrietta, thousands and thousands of miles away..." She stands up, turns away from me and walks out of my bedroom without even kissing me goodnight.

Chapter 13
Not Learning to Read

"It's time for me to teach Henny to read," Nan says. I am excited to hear this because Felicity has told me many times how she loves to read books; it is her favourite thing to do. She says that all the answers to all the questions in the whole world can be found in books.

"Oh, please, Mother, I really do want to learn…"

"No," she says firmly, "I don't want her to learn to read yet, Nan. She is going to be a sucessful artist when she grows up and it's much more important that she learns to draw and paint first. She's starting to learn about colours and their names and how to mix them, which is a very important first step."

Nan looks surprised and I feel confused because I really do want to learn to read.

"Shall I start teaching her ABC's then?"

"No, that's all part of reading. There's lots of time for her to learn her alphabet later on. Instead, I will give her art lessons after tea whenever I am not too busy."

"Do we have enough paper for her to draw on?"

"I will split open some old envelopes and she can draw on the insides to start with. After the War, Henrietta, I will buy you a proper drawing book, but for now we can manage with whatever we can find. As you know I still have my old paint box and some brushes and the utility lead pencils are good for drawing with. I'll teach you everything I know but you have to promise to work very hard and learn as quickly as you can. I don't have a lot of time to spare these days."

Mother tells us that we have to complete the toys by the end of October in order for her to deliver them to Crosby's in time for the Christmas season.

"Oh, Mum, are you sure it is safe for you to go up to London," Nan begins, "what with all the b…."

"Of course it is safe," she replies quickly, "I have to go, I have no choice; I need not only to deliver all the finished toys but to obtain some new orders." Nan looks very worried. I

65

overheard her say to Mother before her last trip to London that she was afraid that she might be killed in the bombing and then she, Nanny, would be left to raise us four children all on her own until the Colonel returned at the end of the War.

"If Nan agrees, and if you behave yourself for the rest of the day and don't ask too many questions, Henrietta, you can stay up this evening to help us work on the toys. Now run outside and play until teatime."

"Nan, I'm just going next door to have a chat with 'Gustus Goat. I haven't talked to him for ages," I confided, "not since yesterday." She tells me to be careful not to fall in the river.

I run down the garden past the cherry trees and through the wild part of the garden and then squeeze behind the huge old tree, which grows beside the river, which is nearly full and there I am, in Miss Jamieson's garden.

'Gustus hears me coming and turns his head towards me. He is such a very handsome goat with a long beard, a ridge of thicker hair down his back and a lock of hair over his forehead. He seems very pleased to see me. I am so glad that Miss Jamieson agreed that I can visit him any time I want. He happily munches the cow parsley I give him whilst I tell him the latest news; about my drawings and the colours and that I am going to be allowed to help make toys later. I stroke him and then brush his coat with an old blue hairbrush that Nanny gave me, which I keep hidden in a hole in the tree. I tell him that one day I will draw a picture of him and he smiles and seems so pleased that, had he been a cat, I know he would have purred. He leans against me fondly and I nearly fall over.

Miss Jamieson comes out of her thatched cottage dressed in her gardening clothes. She stops when she sees me and waves. "How are you? How is Augustus today?" she enquires. "Would you like to come into the Hidden Garden with me and pick some vegetables? I'll give you some to take home."

I give my friend a farewell pat, hide the hairbrush and run to meet her. I love spending time with Miss Jamieson because she is never in a hurry and always appears interested in whatever I have to tell her. My mother never has time to listen to me because she is always much too busy thinking about more important matters.

She brushes aside the curtain of ivy that hides the door, unlatches it and we go inside. There are plants growing in straight rows, some gnarled old apple trees and against the back wall trees that grow flat against the chalk wall with their arms outstretched. They look very strange.

"Whatever is that?" I ask pointing to what looks like a man on a stick.

"That is my scarecrow. I made him myself; I stuffed his face and body with straw and then dressed him up in some old clothes and put him in here. His job is to scare the birds away from

the strawberries but sometimes I think he is sleeping because they still eat most of the ripe ones. There are not many vegetables left at this time of year. Do your family like turnips?" I shake my head, "What about rhubarb?"

"The family love it, but I hate it. Sometimes Nan has to cook it without sugar and it makes my toes curl up."

She chuckles and says, "Well, we had better not send any home with you, had we?" She cuts some curly kale, a cauliflower and some cabbages and puts all the vegetables in her trug. "Come into the kitchen, it is cold out here and it must nearly be your teatime. I'll wrap some of these vegetables up for you to take home to your Nanny." She takes off the outer leaves of the vegetables and I ask her if I can have the trimmings for my rabbits because then it means that I won't have to collect so many sacks of greens.

"I often see you in the street gathering their food. Do you like doing that?" I assure her I do because I love all my rabbits so much that I can't possibly let them go hungry.

"Even if we don't always have quite enough to eat", I confide, "they have to have as much as I can collect because they are all growing so fast."

Miss Jamieson puts the vegetables into an old paper bag and adds some apples. She wraps up the bits and pieces in newspaper and says that she will keep all her scraps for me.

I thank her very much and run home, very pleased with my unexpected gifts. I go into the kitchen and Nan says, "I was just about to call you for tea. What have you got there?" I hand over the paper bag and she opens it. "My goodness me!" she exclaims, laying everything out on the table, "these vegetables are just what we need and, Henny, just look at these lovely rosy-red apples!"

" 'Gustus' mother gave them to me." I explain.

"These are a real treat and dark green vegetables are so good for us these days because they have lots of iron in them."

"Nan," I lower my voice, "She asked me if we wanted any rhubarb but I told her about how it makes my toes curl up when you have to cook it without sugar, so she didn't give us any."

"That's all right, Henny; we just won't mention it." She puts the vegetables in the rack and says that she will make cauliflower cheese for lunch the next day if Mr. Collins has any cheese left in the shop. She hands me an old shopping list and I sit up at the table and draw lots of apples on the back and then colour them.

Mother comes into the kitchen and cries, "What a windfall! By the way, Mr. Watson, the blacksmith says that we can have some horse manure for the vegetable garden. I am wondering how Hugo can bring it home?" She looks at Nan, questioningly.

"No, Mum," Nan replies emphatically, "I will not have manure carried in my pram. Whatever next?"

"Please don't leave, Nanny," I beg, knowing that whenever Mother suggests some especially shocking idea, she always threatens to pack her tin trunk and leave.

"Good gracious!" exclaims my mother, hastily, "Of course I was not thinking of using the pram, Nan! I was just wondering aloud about how Hugo can transport it because it will be so good for the garden."

"Put it in some of those empty sacks that he found in the loft," she suggests, "and then he can tie one on either side of his bike and walk them home."

"What a good idea! Thank you, Nan dear."

Changing the subject she says that it was very kind of Miss Jamieson to send us the fruit and vegetables. "However, I am a little surprised that she did not send us any rhubarb because I am sure that she still has plenty in her garden."

The corners of Nan's mouth twitch, but she does not say a word.

Later that afternoon Lizzybuff is singing to herself in her highchair and Nan and I are laying the table for tea when I tell her that I have to 'go'.

"All right, Henny, run upstairs quickly. Hurry up!"

"Will you come with me, Nan?"

"No, you can manage. Lizzybuff and I will be here waiting for you. I have to finish the ironing before tea."

"What about the Grey Lady? Is she upstairs?"

"Henny stop asking silly questions and just hurry up or else you'll be too late!"

I rush upstairs and run along the landing as fast as I can. The bathroom door is open. I pull down my knickers and climb up and perch on the wooden lavatory seat. I sit there with my eyes closed and think of more rabbit names for the new babies. Suddenly, I am shoved hard and I fall backwards, frantically clutching the edges of the seat to stop myself falling in. My eyes fly open just as Felicity reaches up behind me and pulls the chain. The lavatory flushes copiously, and I think that I have gone right down inside, gone forever. I scream. I am so terrified that I leap off the seat but, because my knickers are still shackling my ankles, I trip and fall and hit my head against the bath and that makes me scream even louder.

"Whatever is happening up there?" Nanny calls from the foot of the stairs. I continue to bawl and Felicity hisses that it serves me right; I should not have dropped her book and spoiled it.

"If you tell Nanny, I'll do it again," she whispers. She returns to her bedroom and quietly closes her door. As soon as she hears Nan running up the stairs she flies out of her room

69

again, rushes into the bathroom and enquires, in her sweetest voice, "Whatever happened to you, Henrietta? You poor little girl!"

Nan arrives in the bathroom and Felicity explains, "I think that she must have fallen off the seat trying to pull the chain…"

Ignoring her, she picks me up and examines the large bruise on my forehead. "That's a nasty bruise," she says, "and I don't see," she says, turning to Felicity, "how she could have pulled the chain, when she could never have reached it."

Felicity looks innocent and shrugs her shoulders, "Maybe she climbed up and slipped?" she suggests.

"Hmmm," says Nanny, thoughtfully, "I believe that there has been some funny business going on here." I sob and hiccup and she hugs me tight whilst gently raising my underwear. "I think that you had better go back into your bedroom, Felicity.

"Come on, Henny, we'll go down to the kitchen and I'll make you a Spam sandwich, that will make you feel better won't it? Just wait until your mother hears about this, Felicity, she will have plenty to say to you, I am sure."

Chapter 14
Toy Making

Nan lights the nursery fire earlier than usual because it is such a chilly day. She suggests that I sit at the table and draw Clementina in her favourite place by the fire. Whilst Lizzybuff is playing with some toys on the nursery floor I notice that she has found an open nappy pin. I watch her as she picks it up, fascinated to see what she will do with it. She crawls up behind the nursing chair where Nan is sitting busily knitting another pair of trousers for Ted. She reaches up and sticks the pin into poor Nan's bottom. The result is amazing. Nan shoots to her feet and her spectacles bounce off her nose. "My goodness me!" she cries. "Whatever was that? Did a bee sting me? Oh, dear, that really did hurt," she says, rubbing her uniform-covered behind. Then, turning around, she sees the nappy pin in Lizzybuff's hand.

"Oh, you naughty little girl!" she exclaims, carefully taking the pin away and closing it. "Well, I never!" She begins to laugh and then picks Lizzybuff up and hugs her. "That was very naughty, sticking a nappy pin into your poor old Nanny! The McPherson children would never have done that! Now, pick up my specs and my sewing, Henny, and we had better go and have some tea."

When we have finished tea I show Mother my drawing and she says it looks just like the cat. I prop Ted up against a pile of books on the table so that he can watch us making toys. The old sewing machine is already on the table and Nan collects the other necessary materials. Mother sits at the machine and sews up a lot of pencil cases from leatherette. When she finishes each one my job is to carefully snip off the ends of cotton with the baby nail scissors and put an eraser, a ruler and some pencils in each of the slots and then fold the case closed. I love being busy and feeling that I am being helpful.

Nan brings out her knitting and finishes a pair of ears for a toy rabbit and then sews them on to his head. Next she pulls some cotton wool out of her knitting bag and stuffs a teddy bear. This one is like my Ted, but not as handsome. He is knitted with army-coloured wool, whereas mine was knitted from reddish-brown string. I choose two buttons for the new teddy's eyes from the button jar, she sews them on and, taking a needle and a length of black wool, she embroiders him a nose. Once she has finished sewing on his ears he looks like a proper teddy bear.

"They say that the War will soon be over, Nan, I hope to goodness that is so. When I am in London I'll see if I can buy  any red, white and blue striped ribbon. It may not be in the shops yet, but I'm sure that it will be available before the War ends. We will make rosettes and sew a small safety pin on the back. I know we'll sell hundreds and hundreds in London. I'll discuss it with Mrs. Gage who buys the bridge pencils, I'm sure she will place a large order. It's a pity I will not have a sample to show her."

"We have a short length of white linen tape left, why don't you paint it in stripes and make one up to show them at the shop?" Nan suggests.

"What a good idea, you are so clever. Bring me the paint box and brushes, Henrietta; they are on the shelf over there. I will pin the tape to the blotter and draw pencil lines on it and then paint the outside ones red and blue."

"Look, Nan, Lizzybuff has fallen asleep on the rug."

"I think I'll leave her there for a while and then take her up to bed when we have finished what we are doing. Cover her up, Henny, with the shawl that's on the nursing chair." I tuck the shawl in tightly all around her, and give our dear little Dormouse a kiss.

"Now we'll let the tape dry and then I'll make it into a rosette. What are you going to knit next?" she asks Nan, "how about another doll? I will make the clothes for her."

"I'm not sure that dolls look good with knitted faces, Mum. If you have one of those fabric faces left, I could knit the whole doll and then you could sew the face on over the knitted face."

"That's another good idea. I think I do have one left. Henrietta, run and bring me Little Janet. Yes, I know it is dark in the drawing room but if you leave this door wide open then you can see her over by the fireplace. Can you carry her? No? All right, I'll come."

She returns with the sewing chest. "There you are, Nan, the very last one. Let me paint the lips a darker red. Why don't you use up that beige wool that we made socks from for the arms and legs and if you don't have enough, you can knit the body in navy blue or whatever colour you have left because it won't show under her frock? I have some black wool for her hair and we can plait it. Henrietta, look in Little Janet and see if you can find some ends of ribbon to make her bows."

Nan searches in her knitting bag for the wool and the doll pattern. Having found some ribbons for her Mother tells me to go into the scullery to fetch a jar of water to wash the paint brushes in.

"Take the torch this time, Henny," Nan says, handing it to me, "I know you can't reach the light switch yet." I hate going out of the nursery in the dark and although I know that our Grey Lady lives upstairs in the linen cupboard most of the time, I never know exactly where she is. Last week she came downstairs.

What happened was this. We were having our Sunday afternoon tea in the drawing room and suddenly the door from the hallway opened and closed. Poor Old Bunker's hackles rose and he got to his feet and growled loudly.

"Well," our mother said, cheerfully, "there she goes - our Grey Lady! Say 'Good afternoon' everyone."

"Good afternoon," we all chorus politely.

There was just time for a grown-up to walk across the floor towards the nursery door, which was opened and then slowly closed. Poor Old Bunker settled down again with a sigh.

"Hugo, please pass me the biscuits. Now, what were we talking about before she interrupted us?"

And that was that, but it did make me feel a bit uneasy.

Mother has assured us that the Grey Lady will never harm us, so there is no reason to fear her or worry about her presence.

Because Hugh had nearly frightened me to death about her already, I never feel quite sure that she truly is a good ghost. However, we usually only hear her footsteps as she paces up and down the upstairs landing.

The sample rosette with a safety pin sewn on the back is complete. "It's not very good, Nan, but I think it will give the impression of what they will look like when they are made up with proper shiny new ribbon, don't you? Now where are we going to find enough safety pins? I only have about a dozen left. I'll ask Miss Emily at Simpson's if she has any next time I go to Patisford. I expect that we will need hundreds and hundreds. Oh dear, this War does makes everything so difficult," she sighs, suddenly looking downcast.

"We'll manage, Mum, we always do," Nan says soothingly. "Let's finish what we are working on and then I'll take Elizabeth up to bed. I'll make supper whilst you and Henny clear up and put away all the toy-making things."

Mother returns from London carrying several boxes. When Nan asks her if she enjoyed herself she beams at her and laughed, in fact she almost giggled.

What is she so happy about, I wonder; she usually seems sad and miserable when she returns from London.

"I went to Lyon's Corner House and had a delicious Welsh Rarebit, it only cost 4d, Nan; I thought that was very reasonable. Then I called on Mrs. Gage, who liked my sample and placed a large order for the rosettes. Everyone in London is talking about the War ending very soon, so we have to make them as quickly as possible. Luckily, I managed to buy a huge quantity of safety pins and look, Nan," she slowly and dramatically opens the box on the table. There, inside, wrapped in crumpled tissue paper is a big heap of very shiny red, white and blue striped ribbon.

"Oh! My goodness me!" exclaims Nanny, "that's really good quality. It will make perfect rosettes, won't it?"

"How many do you think she has ordered?"

"A hundred? Two hundred?"

"No," she hesitates looking slightly worried, "I hardly like to tell you."

"I'll help," I cry eagerly.

"She wants five gross!" she announces triumphantly, unable to keep the good news to herself any longer.

"Five gross? However many is that?"

"Let me see," she uncaps her fountain pen, "that's five times one hundred and forty four. Hand me that envelope, Henrietta. Five times one hundred and forty four is," she pauses and mutters to herself as she adds up the figures, "seven hundred and twenty! Can we ever make that many, Nan?"

"Of course we can; we can work on them on rainy afternoons as well as in the evenings. I am sure that Felicity will help us with them too; she is good with her fingers and she can cut the ribbon into lengths whilst you make the rosettes and sew them together and I will sew on the pins."

"What can I do?" I ask anxiously, feeling that I might get left out of all the excitement.

"You can carefully undo each of the little pins and line them up for Nan to sew on. I will make boxes for the finished rosettes lined with the tissue paper out of the trunks and then I want you to arrange them in neat rows in the boxes."

"Crosby's also placed more toy orders but, luckily, they don't require them until after Christmas. The rosettes will be a lot of work but I'm sure we can manage it and instead of resting on my bed when you take the children out, I will work on them."

Nan looks at her anxiously.

"It is all right, Nan, I can sit in my armchair and put my feet up whilst I make them and I can rest at the same time. It is exciting, darlings, isn't it?" We agree and even Ted looks excited when I ask if they can make him a tiny rosette when the order is finished.

I know that we will have a very happy time making the rosettes and that if I really help a lot, (and don't ask too many questions!) I may get to stay up late every evening.

Chapter 15
The Gypsies

Gypsies come to our village every autumn when they have finished travelling to the different fairs in the county, Mr. Collins told my mother. They usually park their horse-drawn caravans in the shelter of a hedgerow after getting permission from the farmer to set up their campsite on his land. After ensuring that their horses are comfortable, the families settle in for the winter. The women make clothes pegs and carve wooden flowers, which they dye with the juice of berries and then they sell them door to door in the village.

One sunny afternoon there is a knock on the front door. I open it and there are two gypsy women wearing long skirts and shawls both carrying baskets of pegs and flowers. I call my mother to come to see our visitors.

"Good afternoon!" Mother exclaims. She introduces us and enquires kindly, "has it been a good summer for you and your families?" The taller one replies that it had been good on the whole, but that they had run into some trouble on their way to our village.

"Those military people with their red flags, they don't like us traipsing over the Plain anymore, ma'am, and it means we have to go miles out of our way to get here. All those heavy guns and tanks and soldiers, it scares the poor horses you know, and the children," she adds, smiling at me.

"Yes, I am sure it does," Mother agrees. Then she notices a small child hiding behind the other woman's long skirts. "What is your name?" she asks the child. The woman pushes the little girl forward. "Oh! Good heavens!" she gasps, "what on earth is wrong with her arm? Henrietta, run quickly and get Nanny, it looks to me as though it is broken. Did she fall? Whatever happened?"

"We were going along a very bumpy track, trying to keep away from the firing ranges and our caravan went over a rock and Emerald here, fell out of the back." The gypsy puts her basket down beside her on the step.

"Henrietta, I told you to run and ask Nanny to come as soon as she can," my mother snaps.

Nan appears, knitting in hand and catches sight of the child and exclaims, "My goodness me! That arm looks broken. Whatever can we do about it?" she wonders aloud. "I think that we should go into the nursery and I'll tear up some old sheeting to make a bandage. Maybe, Mum, you could find some long flat pieces of kindling in the tool shed? That arm needs a good wash and then setting. Come along, Henny, you can talk to her whilst I see to her poor arm." Nan can become quite bossy when there is an Emergency. The gypsies and I follow her into the nursery. Mother returns with the pieces of wood and then goes upstairs to find an outgrown cardigan of mine for Emerald.

I let Emerald hold Ted's hand while Nanny splints her arm and binds it up with a wide bandage and then makes a sling from a very soft muslin nappy.

"You really should take her to the doctor, you know," she tells Emerald's mother. "I can't set it properly, but it will be more comfortable for her like this in a sling, than just hanging loose by her side. It must pain her dreadfully, poor little mite."

The woman replies, "We never go to doctors, Nanny, but thank you, and you too, ma'am, very much for being so kind to us, most people don't even give us the time of day. Say 'thank you', Emerald, to these ladies. Now we must be on our way. We have lots of pegs to sell, and then we must get back before dark. We are camped way up behind the school."

We return to the front garden and my mother hands the cardigan to Emerald's mother and says that she believes that the child's arm will hurt less if she keeps it warm.

"We need some pegs anyway didn't we, Nan? You said that that when the gypsies come we should buy some. Henrietta, run and get my purse…"

"No, ma'am," says the gypsy. "Please accept some pegs for being so good to my daughter." She picks up her basket, hands the pegs to my mother and, taking Emerald's good hand in hers, walks down the path to the gate. Then she walks back again and says that we will be very welcome to visit them at their campsite anytime. My mother thanks her and says that maybe we will visit them one afternoon.

"Well, she says, "that was lucky they came to our house, wasn't it Nan? That poor child, I'm sure she'll feel better with the arm all done up, don't you?" She gives Nan a quick hug and we go back indoors. She suggests that after tea I draw a picture of the gypsies with their baskets.

Mother decides to come with us on our walk. We both collect flowers, twigs and sprays of old man's beard; she likes teasels very much but she has to pick them herself because they are so prickly. We also pick some giant hog weed, which looks like grown up cow parsley.

When we reach the avenue of horse chestnut trees we slow down and Nan lets Lizzybuff out of the pram so she can run around and get some exercise. No doubt she will collect lots of little stones and even some snails whilst I hunt for the chestnuts that we call conkers. The best ones are still in their half opened prickly shells; they look as though they are smiling. The newborn conkers are shiny and absolutely perfect. It always makes me unhappy to see how quickly they dry out and become dull and wrinkly.

I collect as many as I can and Nan puts them in my crochet bag in the well of the pram away from Lizzybuff's grabby hands, because they are poisonous.

What Hugh does with his conkers is this: he drills holes

 with a gimlet in them and then bakes them in the oven and when they are really well baked he takes them out, lets them cool and then threads a string through the hole and

knots it under the bottom. Now he is ready to fight. The person who breaks the other person's conker first is the winner. I don't like playing this game with him, because it hurts so badly when he hits my hands instead of my conker accidentally-on-purpose, and then calls me a sissy if I cry. He says that he is going to find a small chestnut tree and plant it in our garden and then, when it grows big, we will have our own conkers. I hope he will let me have some.

Nan says, "The afternoon is drawing in, Mum, I think we should go home now, the dew is beginning to fall and I don't want Henrietta and Elizabeth catching their death because, as you know, in a damp house like ours colds can quickly develop into bronchitis."

Nan calls Lizzybuff and lifts her up to put her back in the pram. However, she struggles and wriggles so hard that Nan has to put her down. "Me walk, Nanny!" she declares and runs towards the road. Nan grabs her and tells her that if she behaves she will make her special Marmite sandwiches for tea. This quietens her down because these are her favourites. We finally head for home and when we get there I take my bag of conkers out of the pram and take them into the nursery.

Mother calls me and asks me to pick the last of the wallflowers in the garden because they will give our arrangement some colour. We put them, and our leafy treasures, in the golden glass vase, which she keeps on the windowsill at the far end of the hallway. As the sun sets, the rays shine through the vase and it glows.

"Later, Henrietta, I will make a drawing of it and tomorrow you can paint it." I thank her and meanwhile I try to draw the gypsy ladies and Emerald with her arm in the sling.

As the weather begins to change and it becomes colder, we go for shorter walks. Some afternoons we work on the rosettes and other afternoons my mother gives me drawing lessons. She says she wants to teach me something called 'p'spectif', whatever that is, when I am a little bit older. I am very happy learning to be an artist and when I am having my lessons no one else is allowed to interrupt, which makes me feel that she loves me and that I am important.

Chapter 16
Market Day

I am excited because I am going on the bus with Mother to Patisford to shop. Hugh is coming too to sell some of our pet rabbits at the Saturday Market.

Briggs decides which rabbits should go to market and this time he has chosen Michael and Sophia, a fluffy grey lady rabbit. He is also sending Sandy, a big bad-tempered brown one because he bit me so I am not sad to see him go but I will miss the other two. Briggs says that there will soon be so many babies that if we don't sell some we will have rabbits everywhere, which makes me laugh as I imagine baby rabbits all over the house, all over the roof, all over the garden, all over the whole wide world.

Hugh puts straw in the bottom of each box and a handful of fresh dandelion leaves so that the rabbits can eat their breakfasts whilst we are on the bus and it will keep them busy and stop them missing their families so much.

Briggs lifts each rabbit out of their cage by its ears. He promises me that this does not hurt them and, as they never squeal, he must be right. Hugh holds the first box open and Briggs put Sophia into it, after first letting me give her a goodbye stroke and a kiss, and then Sandy, who struggles and kicks and makes a fuss. He quickly closes the box and holds it shut whilst Briggs ties it up with string. He then puts Michael in the second box after I have said a sorrowful goodbye to him. Hugh ties up that box. We always use the same pieces of string because that is all we have and there is no more in the shops. It is now my brother's job to look after my rabbits and to make sure they get to market and to bring the string safely home again.

We catch the after-breakfast bus and Mother, who is getting really rather plump, climbs the stairs slowly, puffing as she pulls herself up by the handrail. I wonder why she is getting fat when she gives most of her food to us. Clementina is getting fatter and fatter every day but then she catches and eats lots of rats.

Surely she doesn't......? No, of course not!

I scramble up onto the top deck and Hugh follows carrying one box while Briggs carries the other. He puts it down on Hugh's seat and then rushes back downstairs and jumps off the bus before it starts up. We settle ourselves comfortably in the front seat with Hugh and the rabbits on the seat behind us. Briggs stands at the bus stop and I wave goodbye to him and he smiles up at me and waves back. After Nan and Ted, Briggs really is my next best friend.

Mother is wearing her pale brown fur coat and her favourite silk Paisley headscarf tied under her chin. (I decide to use that name for one of the next lot of baby rabbits, if I can remember it). I have on my blue winter coat, which she made from a very soft blanket we had been given by one of our great aunts. She told me that our granny is the eldest of eleven and her husband, our grandfather, had been one of a family of seventeen. That is the reason, she says, that we have so many great aunts, great uncles and all sorts of other relatives, although neither family is RC, she adds, somewhat mysteriously. My coat is very warm and I like the feel of it; it is a bit fluffy but not so fluffy that the fluff gets up my nose. Hugh, who never feels the cold, is wearing his school mackintosh.

Our sandwiches and the gas masks sit in the basket on the seat beside me. We have to carry them in case there is a surprise gas attack. I gaze out of the window and wonder what a gas attack is. What does it look like? Is it big? Will it attack me, or does it only attack Grown-Ups? Will it knock me down when it attacks me? How long will I be able to wear my mask before I can't breathe any more?

If I can't breathe any longer, I will be dead. I know this because one day I found a feathery bird lying on the lawn and I took it indoors to Nan who said that it had stopped breathing and so it was dead. She told me to take it out of the house at once because it might have germs, and then come back in to have my hands washed. Would I have germs if I stopped breathing and became dead? If I did, she wouldn't love me any more because she always says that the two things she hates most in this world are germs and cows. If Nan didn't love me any more whatever would I do? I feel like crying but instead snuggle up against my mother who puts her furry arm around my shoulders. I pretend that I am being hugged by a very large pale brown rabbit.

Once I have managed to change the subject in my mind I sit up and look out over the Downs. Our seat on top of the bus is so high up that we can see far across the countryside. When the bus passes through the villages I look down into people's gardens. Most of the gardens look sad and ugly because it is still wintertime and no one takes much notice of them, but I am not too unhappy about this because Nan told me that soon winter will be over and that spring, and the warm weather, will arrive. Then all sorts of new things will happen; plants will spring up, the grass will grow longer and children will play out of doors again. People will put their washing on the line, which will flutter in the breeze instead of freezing as stiff as boards like Nanny's Flags do.

We used to take Poor Old Bunker on the bus with us, but one day he was sick all over the floor, and the bus conductor was very cross and said he would not have a dog travelling on his bus who did not know how to behave. Now he has to stay at home with Clementina and the rabbits.

We are half way to Patisford when my brother turns around to make faces at a young boy who is sitting at the back of the bus. Whilst he is busy doing this, the box that he tied up flies open and Michael Rabbit wriggles out and tears off down the aisle, down the stairs, and leaps off the open platform into a field. Hugh rings the bell frantically and calls out to the conductor to ask the driver to stop the bus at once so that he can run and catch the rabbit. "The only rabbit I'll stop to catch is one for my tea," the conductor tells Hugh, who by then was downstairs.

My heart stops. Michael must be in great danger. Then I notice that he has raced right across the field towards a large group of wild rabbits, a long way away from the bus and the busy main road.

"I've a good mind to take sixpence off your pocket money, Hugo," Mother tells him crossly, when he returns, huffing and puffing. He plonks himself down on the seat beside the empty box looking very distressed.

"Will Michael Rabbit be all right, Mummy?" I ask.

"Oh, yes, Henrietta,' she replies. "He will go and live with his country cousins and have a most enjoyable time." I feel a bit better because, with his shiny black fur and his long white

82

whiskers, he is very good looking, and, as she always says, it is the good looking people who do so much better in this world than the plain ones. I promise myself I will look for him every time we pass that field.

From the Bus Station we walk to the Market Place, which is very crowded with people milling around buying and selling fruits and vegetables, cups and saucers, pots and pans, bundles of firewood, second-hand clothes and all sorts of different interesting things. We walk past the stalls into the Cattle Market, so that I can see the sheep, lambs, cows and calves. They all jostle and push each other, their breath clouding the chilly morning air. Elderly farmers lean against the wooden hurdles, discussing them. They have to shout to be heard above the noise. Several young women, in green jumpers, jodhpurs and knee socks, are helping with the animals. My mother explains that, because all the young men have gone to war, these young women were ordered to leave their office work in London and join the Land Army and then sent down to the countryside to work on the farms.

She tells Hugh to make sure he does not lose his gas mask and that he has to wait in the rabbit section, until our remaining two are sold. "I don't need the box back but remember to keep the string, Hugo," she says. "After they are sold you can stay in the Market, but don't lose the money from selling the rabbits, and don't spend any of it. I want every penny," she adds, "especially, after you let the black one escape. Meet us at half past three at the Bus Station so we can all travel home together."

Hugh, although he says that when he grows up he wants to be a soldier like our Father, or a boxer, really wants to be a farmer and loves to spend hours looking at the animals and talking to the farmers. As we hurry off I turn to wave to him but he is already discussing something with an old shepherd, who is pointing at one of the sheep with his crook.

Chapter 17
Secret Goings-on

What a treat! I have Mother all to myself until it is time to go home. We turn into one of the narrow side streets and climb up the steps into the silversmith's shop. I enjoy helping clean our silver so I am always interested to see all the various teapots, tea sets, jugs, mugs, tankards and platters that are on display. My mother walks up to the counter at the back of the store and speaks to the silversmith. She takes a parcel out of her bag and hands the cigarette lighter from the drawing room to him. He examines it closely through a funny sort of glass that he puts up against his eye.

"Is it going to be mended?" I ask.

"Yes," she replies.

Whilst the Grown-Ups carry on a quiet conversation, I discover a large platter on one of the lower shelves. By kneeling down on the rug and moving from side to side my reflected face changes in a most fascinating way.

"Are we going to collect the candlesticks that you left to be mended last time?" Taking no notice of my question, she quickly thanks the old man and we leave the shop.

I think that she has sold the candlesticks and the lighter as well to pay the school fees and to feed us all. However, I know when it is best not to ask.

I am so glad that I don't have a problem with feeding the rabbits because there is so much rabbit food in our village and it is all free. How difficult it would be if I had to cope with lots and lots of Rabbit Ration Books. How many coupons would it be for each sack of cow parsley? Would each rabbit have to have their own Ration Book . . ?

"Henrietta, you are daydreaming again, now hurry up, we still have lots more shopping to do." She takes my hand and we head for the wool shop, where she asks the assistant for six ounces of baby wool. She seems quite vague when I ask her what Nan will knit with it, and, changing the subject, she tells me names of the coloured wools the shop will stock once the War is over. "Raw umber, crimson, emerald green, the purples - winter purple is blue based and summer purple is red based, and there is cerulean, raw sienna, sepia, and many more." I am enchanted with these magical colours. Because it is Wartime the shop only stocks boring colours like black, white, and grey and, of course, lots of army-coloured wool for soldiers' socks.

We hurry past St. Francis' Church and into the chemist's shop. She smiles nervously at the chemist, and says that she requires a rubber hot water bottle.

"Now Mrs. Rowansforde, you know that, with all the rubber being used for the War Effort, I can only sell you a rubber hot water bottle if you are pregnant and you have a letter from your doctor stating that it is so."

"What does 'pregnant' mean?" I ask.

"Be quiet, Henrietta," she said, sounding very annoyed.

She hands him an envelope and he goes into the back room and returns with an orange hot water bottle, which he wraps in newspaper and hands to her. "Is that for me? Can I have it instead of the nasty old stone one which burns my toes? It keeps falling out of the end my bed and it wakes Nan up when it hits the floor."

"Do be quiet, child," Mother repeats, snappily. I decide that I had better be quiet or she will tell Nan that I have been a nuisance and then I might not get to go shopping with her again for a very long time, maybe for years and years. She says that she is tired and that she wants to sit down for a while. I am pleased because although Nan says that I am a very good walker for my age I also get tired sometimes. I ask her if we can have our elevenses at my favourite teashop and she agrees. We cross another street and there it is, the Ginger Cat Teashop! She says that that is not its real name but that is what I call it.

She opens the door, and there he is ... the Ginger Cat himself. He has been waiting for me. I am about to follow him when I catch sight of a tall jar on the counter. "Oh, look, are those sweets, Mother?" I point to a jar on the counter filled with long, shiny, golden coloured sticks.

"Yes, those are barley sugar twists, but no,

86

you can't have any," she replies firmly.

"Don't we have enough coupons?"

"Yes, Henrietta, but we cannot buy them," she lowers her voice, "because," she pauses dramatically, "they have all been poisoned by Hitler."

"Does Nan know about it?"

"Yes, Henrietta, of course Nanny knows, every Grown-Up knows.... Now come along, it is time for elevenses."

The Ginger Cat, followed by an elderly waitress, leads us to our table. I kneel down on the floor beneath it and tell him all about Michael's amazing escape. He doesn't seem alarmed by my tale, which is reassuring. I stroke his back and he purrs loudly. He really is the handsomest ginger gentleman cat that I have ever met and he is so much bigger and stronger than our own little lady cat, Clementina. I wish I could take him home to meet her.

The waitress brings our meagre order; a pot of tea for my mother, a glass of water for me and a piece of toast and margarine for each of us. At home we have big butter week and little butter week and then eat margarine when we finish our butter ration. We each have our own butter dishes and nobody is allowed to eat anybody else's ration. We children are not allowed to drink tea; either it isn't in our ration books or else it is too expensive. We finish our elevenses and my mother pays the waitress whilst I say good-bye to my ginger friend.

"Pick up my parcels, Henrietta, it is time to go. We will go to Simpson's next and then to the Abbey." Little did I know what a horrible tale I was about to overhear.

Chapter 18
Simpson's

We walk down the High Street until we come to a tall, narrow, black and white building squeezed between two larger ones. For the first time I notice the old green signboard over the shop door. The gold letters are cracked and faded. I ask her to tell me what it says and she reads:

SIMPSON'S
Drapers, Milliners & Haberdashers
Established 1793

Before I can ask her what the lovely words mean she hurries up the worn stone steps and as she opens the door the bell jangles to welcome us.

After the bright sunlight outside, it is very dark and gloomy inside the shop. Shadowy bolts of blackout and other dull-coloured material lie on the shelves. Orderly rows of elderly remnants rest on a table just inside the door. An empty sewing thread display case reminds customers of better, more prosperous days. Mannequins, discreetly draped in dustsheets, are huddled together in one corner. Mother says that they are all waiting patiently for the end of the War when they will once more be dressed in the manner to which they were accustomed. Battered-looking, dust-covered felt hats in sad shades of black, grey and dark blue, sit lopsidedly on stands of different heights on one of the empty counters.

"Good morning ladies, what can we do for you today, Mrs. Rowansforde?" enquires the tall, thin Simpson sister, Miss Dorothy. Miss Emily, who is short, and bird-like in her movements, smiles from behind the till. They are both dressed in black and wear necklaces of jet beads. They look pale, tired and sad. I wonder who has died because my mother once told me that people only wear jet beads when someone in the family is dead.

Mother replies that she requires several yards of silk cord to finish some of her handwork before taking the completed orders up to London to the toyshop. We follow Miss Dorothy to the back of the shop, where she pulls back tattered, faded velvet curtains, which might once have been blue, and leads us into the stock room, our footsteps ringing on the bare floorboards. Many boxes of different sizes are piled up on the shelves and on top of several empty, disused glass counters. Mote-filled rays of sunlight struggle through the cobwebby, leaded panes of a tall, narrow window.

Miss Dorothy opens a big cupboard and brings out a large box. She removes the lid with a flourish, and, to my mother's delight and astonishment, there is an array of colourful ribbons, braids, edgings, piping, silken cords, tassels and a variety of different kinds of lace.

"They are all fine pre-War stock," Miss Dorothy proclaims proudly. "These days we don't have much call for trimmings of such quality, and I don't suppose that, even when the War is over, we'll ever see quality goods like this again." They stand together, Mother, plump in her fur coat and Miss Dorothy, thin in her ancient black frock, as though observing a few moments of silence in memory of pre-War quality.

I follow them back into the main shop. Mother stops suddenly and I bump into her furry behind. "Careful, Henrietta, you nearly knocked me down." She turns to Miss Dorothy and says, "I nearly forgot something very important. Do you", she pauses, and Miss Dorothy looks expectantly at her, "do you," she repeats, "have any small gold safety pins? I need hundreds - at least two gross, if you have them."

"Let's go back into the shop and ask my sister if she knows

if there are any hidden away in one of the boxes."

Miss Emily kindly suggests that I climb up onto the chair and then up onto the counter to play with the buttons whilst her sister hunts through box after box for the safety pins. Finally she cries out in triumph and produces two small bunches and puts them on the counter by the till. Mother thanks her, although she looks disappointed that she has found so few.

Whilst Miss Emily measures out our purchases, I sit beside the large shiny, black Chinese bowl, which has a pattern of flowers painted on the outside. It is full of hundreds and hundreds of buttons. Over the years, every time there was an odd button left over from a set, Miss Emily had explained, they put it in the bowl, as their mother, grandmother and great grandmother had done before them. So, she said that some of the buttons were very, very old and very valuable. Every time we go into the shop, the old lady says that I can take out the ones I like best and line them up in rows on the counter. If she is not busy she will tell me what each of my chosen ones are made of. The smooth, cool-feeling ones are made of either glass or china, while the really cold ones are metal, sometimes of brass and sometimes of silver or copper. Others are silk-covered or made of ivory, whalebone, wood or shell. I run my hands through the bowl and search for my favourites; the one shaped like a butterfly, which is made of silver, the fish-shaped one carved from ivory and the tiny enamelled red ladybird. I wriggle out of my shoes and let them drop to the floor.

Meanwhile, Miss Emily measures out the ribbon and cord and rings them up in the till. She apologizes for putting them in a used brown paper bag, "It's the War", she remarks, "we are so short of everything. Well, you know all about that, don't you ma'am? And how is Nanny?"

"She's at home looking after Lizzybuff," I inform her.

"Nanny is well, thank you," Mother replies, ignoring my interruption, "but that reminds me," she leans closer to Miss Emily, and asks in a confidential whisper (even though there are no other customers in the shop) "she has run out of elastic for Henrietta's and Elizabeth's knickers. Do you, by chance, have a yard or so to spare?" I feel so embarrassed at having my underwear discussed in public that I accidentally knock one of the buttons off the counter and it rolls across the floor and under the remnants' table. I scramble down and manage to retrieve it, a clear blue glass one, which I especially prize.

"I'm sorry, Mrs. Rowansforde, I would love to oblige a special customer like you, but not even an inch. We haven't had any for months, maybe not for years."

I sneeze loudly and Mother turns away from the counter and catches sight of me emerging from under the table.

"In Heaven's name, whatever are you doing, Henrietta? Get up at once. And where are your shoes? Look at your clean socks, whatever will Nanny say when she sees how grubby you have made them? And," she gasps, "just look at your best winter coat. It's ruined. I can't turn my back on you for one minute without you getting into trouble."

"I dropped one of the special buttons," I explain, "but I found it," I smile at her and the sisters and hold up the button for them to see. I then reach up on tiptoe and put the button back in line with the others.

She orders me to pick up my shoes and to climb back up on the counter. She brushes the dust off my coat with her hand and then brushes the soles of my socks really hard, so that my feet feel very hot and then puts on my shoes and laces them up so tightly that they pinch. She orders me to put all the buttons back in the bowl.

Both the sisters look distressed and apologize for the dusty state of the floor and of the shop in general. Miss Dorothy then clears her throat and asks Mother nervously, "Did my sister tell you our terrible news?" She twists the beads of her necklace with her claw-like arthritic fingers. Mother replies that she has not. Miss Dorothy moves a few paces to the left behind the counter and my mother follows on the shop side. I concentrate hard on putting the buttons very slowly back into the bowl, one by one, whilst appearing not to listen to the Grown-Ups' conversation.

I catch phrases of the awful tale. "...Our great-niece Ellen,

… direct hit, not a chance… husband killed in France last year …two dear little girls. Gone … bombed… all three killed … only relatives… wanted her to take over… no family left … too old…. end of our tether…"

Mother makes soothing noises and pats the old lady's shoulder kindly. Although I do not know Ellen and her family, I still feel as though I am going to be sick and my tummy aches and I long for Nanny and Ted to be there to comfort me.

"I apologize, ma'am," Miss Dorothy says, making an effort to pull herself together and moving back along the counter, "for burdening you with our sorrows and problems, I know how difficult it must be for you and Nanny to manage, what with the Colonel being away, and you with four young children. But, since our brother died three years ago, we have had no one to help us, and no one to advise us. We had hoped Ellen and her husband would take over here at the end of the War, such a helpful young couple they were. We're getting on you know, and excuse my bad manners for mentioning our ages, but Emily is eighty seven and losing her sight and I am nearly eighty four. It's all getting to be too much for us. No young people around, just us old ones left to cope as best we can. Maybe we'll retire when the War is over. It will be very sad," she says, her voice cracking, "because our family has been in business in this very shop for more than 150 years," she sniffs and blows her nose on her lace-trimmed hanky.

Mother sympathizes and tells them that, with Mr. Churchill in charge, everything will soon get better and, once the War is over, life will become easier.

Picking up her parcels she says, "We must hurry on now as we want to go to the Abbey before we catch the ten-to-four bus home. I will say a prayer for you both. Come along Henrietta, climb down and say good-bye. We will see you again soon, Miss Dorothy and Miss Emily."

"God bless you ma'am", Miss Emily says, "and you too, Miss Henrietta."

"God bless you too," she replies. I slide off the counter and bravely smile goodbye to the old ladies trying not to cry at the snippets of their terrible news that I had overheard.

We climb down the steps, and as mother closes the door behind her, the bell jangles farewell. Back out in the street, I am surprised to see that the sun was still shining because the War had indeed cast a very dark shadow on the sunny day.

Chapter 19
The Abbey

Two injured dolls lie in the window of the old Doll's Hospital waiting patiently for first aid once the War is over. This is when Mother says that she expects the elderly lady who owns it will re-open the Hospital.

When I was much younger I had a china doll named Pippa; she had pink cheeks and blue eyes and I loved her very much. One day I tripped on the back step of our old house and cut my chin open. I screamed and, frightened at seeing my blood dripping on the step, I dropped her. I can still remember the terrible noise of my beloved baby shattering into smithereens. No one, not even the old lady could have put my baby back together again. Nanny helped me wrap the pieces in an old woolly jacket, put them into a small shoebox and we buried her broken remains in the garden. I felt very unhappy about leaving her little grave when we moved to this new house and I have never, ever wanted a china doll since.

We hurry through St. Botolph's Gate into the Abbey Gardens. My mother takes my hand, sensing, perhaps, that I had heard more than I should have. I cheer up when I see high up in the sky the big fat, shiny, silver barrage balloon which she tells me is protecting the Abbey from being bombed.

We follow the pathway across the overgrown lawns to the Abbey door; it seems that not even God can get his grass mown very often in Wartime.

The Abbey is huge, full of echoes and very cold, and even the afternoon sun shining through the stained-glass windows and making coloured patterns on the stone floors does not make it any warmer.

We kneel down in a pew to say our prayers. Mine is always the same:

"Please God, stop the War and let there be Peace and don't let our father be killed and please bless Mummy, Nanny and Briggs. Please Lord God, bless me and Ted, Clementina, Poor Old Bunker and Augustus and all the rabbits and all the animals in the whole wide world. Amen."

Mother rises to her feet and we slowly walk up the aisle

towards the dark screen behind which God lives, past the tombs of famous saints and knights and ladies, who, instead of going to heaven, had been turned to stone. One day she told me that some of them had been there for hundreds and hundreds of years. Even their clothes and armour are stone. What had they done to be turned to stone? I couldn't ask my mother because talking is not allowed in the Abbey because it was where God lives and it is rude to talk in His house.

The organ begins to play and the music swells and resounds around the old building. Surely it is loud enough to wake even those who have been turned to stone?

The Lord God, God's younger brother, lives behind the altar in the side chapel. He is the one who makes, and then looks after, all the animals whilst God is busy running the rest of the world. I like the Lord God best and love His special hymn:

> *"All things bright and beautiful*
> *All creatures great and small*
> *All things wise and wonderful*
> *The Lord God made them all."*

The choir start practising and their voices soar and echo right up into the roof. The sound makes me feel like crying and when I look up at my mother I see that she has tears in her eyes.

When they have finished singing we return to the pew and kneel down. I repeat my same prayer, but this time I remember to include the Ginger Cat in my list. I know that it is a good thing to say our prayers often, it helps keep us safe. As we leave the Abbey, the wind slams the heavy door shut behind us.

It is getting much colder so we hurry through the town to the bus station where Hugh is waiting for us and when the bus arrives we clamber up on top. I soon fall asleep, worn out from so much walking.

Mother shakes me awake saying that we have arrived home. I am sad that I have slept so deeply that I have missed looking for Michael Rabbit, even though it is nearly dark. We get off the bus and there is dear Nan waiting for us at the garden gate with a welcoming smile. She tells us that Felicity has made ginger biscuits for tea and is now studying in her room, and that she and

Lizzybuff have had a quiet day.

That night I lie in bed holding Ted tight in my arms. There is only the glimmer from the nightlight to dispel my awful fear of the dark. The parts of the dreadful story that I had overheard that afternoon in the shop about Ellen and the little girls all being killed keep running over and over in my mind.

Who can I tell about this – tell how upset I am? I have heard stories, or at least snippets of such stories, before but this time the old ladies' grief is engraved upon my soul.

If I tell my mother, she will scold me for eavesdropping.

If I tell Nan, I know that she will comfort me but that Mother will make her tell her what I had said, and then she will be cross that I had not confided in her first.

Felicity is far too grown up to be interested in my childish fears and worries.

Hugh will either threaten to tell my mother or laugh and call me a sissy.

Lizzybuff is far too young to tell my woes to.

Briggs would understand but he has already gone home.

That only leaves Ted, Doggie and the motley crew of other toys that share my bed. I can tell them anything but all they do is stare back at me. They don't even smile or purr at me like the Ginger Cat or waffle their furry noses at me like the rabbits.

The story runs through my head again and I start to weep quietly under the bedclothes. I bury my face in Doggie and make him thoroughly damp.

Suddenly I hear Nan say, "Whatever is the matter, Henny?" I pop out from under the blankets, and there she is, so reassuring, so loving and so concerned. "Why are you crying?"

I only wished that I could have told her the truth.

"I've got toothache," I fib, sobbing hard.

She leans over and hugs me. "Now you snuggle right down and I'll cover you up and then I'll tell you a…"

"Nan, there's something warm and fluffy in the bottom of my bed! I can feel it with my toes…"

"It's probably one of your toys. I don't know how you manage to sleep with…"

"No, Nan, it's wriggling!"

"Let me pull back the bedclothes." She does and we both gasp with astonishment. There, right at the bottom of my bed, is Clementina with a heap of tiny little kittens.

"Well, I never!" she exclaims. "Fancy that! Did you ever see anything like it?"

"Can they stay there? I'll lie very still and I won't squash them. Please, please let me keep them here."

"No Henny! Of course not! Now jump into my bed and I will change your sheets when I come back. I'll find a basket to put the kittens in and put it beside the kitchen range where they will be warm. I'll give the cat a saucer of milk too, she may be thirsty. No, don't touch them; she will let you touch them when they are a bit bigger."

"Nan, how many are there?" She holds up one hand with fingers outspread.

"Where did she get them from?" I ask.

"Henrietta, no more questions! Just be quiet whilst I deal with the kittens. How is your toothache?"

"Better, thank you."

Kittens! My own special furry babies!

One frosty afternoon Mother says that it is time for us to print the Christmas wrapping paper before she gets too busy with other Christmassy things such as making sure that Hugo goes up to the woods to collect some holly to decorate the drawing room with. When I ask her if we can make some paper chains she says we can't because she has no coloured paper left.

First she cuts some raw potatoes in half and carves a design on each one. There's a Christmas tree, a star, Father Christmas' face and a holly leaf, then she shows me how to dip each one into poster paint, let the extra paint run off and then stamp the design on the roll of shelf paper.

The doll's pram is beside me as I work at the nursery table and she is about to tell me something when her attention is drawn to the pram. "Henrietta, what is that moving under the covers?" she asks.

"Clementina's kittens. She asked me to look after them whilst she goes and looks for the other's that are lost," I reply.

"She had this many," I hold up my hand with fingers outstretched, "and now she only has these." I hold up both my thumbs. "Where did they go?"

"I have no idea," she replies, "but if you cover them up so tightly, they will die. Turn back the covers so they can breathe and move that old mauve rabbit to one side. Yes, that is better."

We go back to our printing. When I hear Clementina meowing at the door I let her in. As she jumps into the pram, I remove Ted and the rabbit and she snuggles down to feed her remaining kittens, purring like an engine.

Chapter 20
It's Christmastime!

"It's Christmas Eve, Henny! Get out of bed quickly; we want to show you something. Put on your dressing gown and your slippers because it is bitterly cold. Now climb up on the chair in front of the window." Nan turns to Mother and asks her if she should wake Elizabeth.

"No," said replies, "let her sleep; she will enjoy it more next year. Maybe the Big Ones would like to watch? Will you go and wake them for me, Nan?" She returns saying that Felicity is already watching from her window but that Hugh is so fast asleep she can't wake him up.

Mother switches off the light, Nan pulls back the curtains and the blackout and opens the window just enough for us to hear them singing *'O Little Town of Bethlehem…'* It is magical. Then, *'Good King Wenceslas'* followed by my mother's favourite; *'I Saw Three Ships come sailing in on Christmas Day in the Morning…'*

When they have finished, Mother opens the window wider and a flurry of big snowflakes rush in. She calls out to the singers and invites them to come into the kitchen and warm themselves. As she shuts the window Felicity joins us and we all hurry downstairs.

We greet them at the front door and they stamp their feet on the doormat to get the snow off their shoes and then troop down the hallway, through the scullery into the kitchen. Nan boils the kettle and makes cocoa for everyone; she even makes me a small cup. Mother had made a big cake for Christmas Day and some tiny cakes out of berries, fruits and nuts that we had gathered in the hedgerows some time before.

The carol singers (who are really the butcher, the baker, the grocer, the postman and their wives, all members of the church choir) warm themselves by the kitchen range as they sip cocoa and eat the little cakes, which Felicity hands around. Mother takes Mr. Collins aside and explains that she had recently received Granny's sugar ration in the post, and that is how she has been able to make the cakes. I heard her tell Nan earlier that she was going to explain this to him in case he thought that she was buying sugar on the black market, wherever that is.

"Thank you very much on behalf of us all," says Mr. Collins, who is also the choirmaster, "Thank you, ma'am, and you too, Nanny. That was a very welcome warm-up. Now, just before we go on our way, out into the cold and snow like Good King Wenceslas and his page," he chuckles, "let us sing one special verse for young Miss Henrietta here and her teddy bear." They sing '*Away in a manger...*' I am enchanted and feel so happy that we live in The Old Manor Farmhouse. Amidst laughter and chatter and lots of Christmas good wishes, they leave. I help tidy up the kitchen and then we go to bed.

I climb up onto the chair once more and peep through the blackout. The village street is empty and the snow has already covered the carol singers' footprints. At that moment, a black cat runs out from the hedge and crosses the road.

"Nan," I turn away from the window, "I'm worried. There's a black pussycat out there all by himself. Where do you think he's going in the middle of the night? Will he be all right? Will he get lost? Is he looking for Clementina's lost kittens?"

"Henny, close the blackout, climb down off that chair, get into your bed and go to sleep. You and your animals, I don't know, it's all you ever think about - cats, rabbits, goats, kittens and mice. It's the middle of the night and you are still asking questions. It is Christmas Day tomorrow... " she starts, but before she can continue I interrupt her.

"If we stay awake all night will Ted and I see Father Christmas? He will come down our chimney, won't he, Nan?"

"Now, Henrietta," she says, sternly, (she never calls me Henrietta unless she is very cross with me), "I woke you up to listen to the carols as a special treat, so go to sleep and never mind waiting up to see Father Christmas. All good little girls, and good teddy bears, are fast asleep when he comes." I snuggle down in my bed and quickly fall asleep, exhausted from all the excitement.

My eyes fly open and I know that, at last, it is Christmas Day. I jump out of bed but it is so bitterly cold I jump right back in again and pull up all my blankets up under my chin. I wonder if Nan is awake.

"Nan," I whisper.

"Yes, Henny," she whispers back, "put your dressing gown on and then run as quickly as you can and jump into my bed."

"My goodness!" she remarks as I wriggle my way in, "you feel very frosty! It really is a bitterly cold morning. Happy Christmas!" She gives me a hug. "Did you enjoy the carols last night?"

"Oh, yes, Nan. Thank you for waking me up. I wonder if that pussycat is alright. Do you think he is?"

She ignores my question and says, "I think that I had better wash and dress you and Elizabeth in front of the kitchen fire, it is far too cold up here. Snuggle down for a few minutes while I get dressed and go down to make sure the kitchen is warm. I'll take your clothes with me and put them in the oven and if it is not too hot it will warm them up nicely."

I fall back to sleep and dream of carol singers, cats, kittens and Christmas. "Come on, Henny, wake up! The kitchen is now warm enough so I will see to you first and then I'll wake the Little One later." She puts on my slippers and, leaving Lizzybuff fast asleep, we hurry downstairs. It is so cold our breath looks like smoke. Nanny washes me with warm water from the big kettle because the pipes are frozen solid. "I'll have to ask Hugh to collect some snow in the biggest saucepan and then I can melt it on the range." She helps me into my best red velvet frock with a lace collar that had been passed down to us by one of our cousins.

"Can you start laying the table for breakfast, please? I will go up and get Elizabeth. Close the doors quickly after me because we don't want to let the cold air in from the hallway do we? I will light the fires in both the nursery and the drawing room today. I don't remember such a cold morning for many years, there must have been a heavy frost on top of the snow." She goes out and I close the door behind her and start laying the table.

Christmas Day! At last!

The door opens and Mother comes in wearing her winter coat and silk scarf. "Are you going out?" I ask her.

"Happy Christmas, dearest!" she cries. "No, I am not, but

it is such a freezing morning I need my coat on until the house warms up. It has become much colder since the carol singers left last night. Did you enjoy listening to them? I did, and they loved my little Christmas cakes." She looks down and exclaims, "Just look at the brick floor, it's covered in frost!"

Nan arrives with a very sleepy and tousled Lizzybuff tucked under one arm and a bundle of clothing under the other. Mother says that she will dress her if Nan will go and wake up the Big Ones.

"Don't stand any nonsense from Hugo, Nan, make him get up, and Felicity too. We want to get on with breakfast so that we can open our presents."

Hugh and Felicity come into the kitchen and she announces that the pipes are frozen.

"I know. Happy Christmas to you both!" She goes to hug them and Hugh manages to wriggle free just in time. "Let's have breakfast now; Felicity, please put Elizabeth in the highchair, and Hugo, I'll switch off the light and you open the window and the grab the milk churn." A blast of cold air rushes into the darkened room as Hugh, grunting and groaning, heaves the heavy churn up over the windowsill onto the floor and then closes the window

"My hands are frozen solid," Hugh complains, switching the light back on.

"Come by the range and warm them," Nan suggests. "If it is still this cold tomorrow maybe you should put your gloves on. We don't want you getting frost bite, do we? Mum, I do believe the milk is frozen solid too, like a big ice cream!" We laugh as she and Hugh struggle to move the churn closer to the fire to melt the milk for our corn flakes.

(One day we had finished all the milk and then found a big slithery surprise on the bottom of the empty churn - a very large slug. Mother was furious and complained to the farmer, who sent us a big bag of free potatoes to make up for it.)

Once we finish breakfast and have washed up, we all hurry into the warm drawing room and there is our Christmas tree. It is actually the top of the old yew tree that Briggs cut off. There are lots of small parcels hanging from the drooping branches and some larger ones arranged underneath it all wrapped in the paper

that we printed. My mother and Nan agreed that they did not want us to give them presents this year but as soon as the War is over we will all have lots of presents every Christmas.

Mother goes over to the tree and we make ourselves comfy on the chairs and the sofa. Lizzybuff sits on Nan's knee and Ted sits on mine. Felicity chooses the big armchair by the roaring fire and Hugh paces up and down, impatiently. One after another, Mother takes presents off the tree or from underneath it. I wait anxiously to hear my name called. "Felicity, with love from Nanny." She opens her present and finds that Nan has knitted her a long dark blue scarf. She thanks her and gives her a hug. Then it's Hugh's turn. My mother has built him another tunnel out of cardboard for his train set. He is so thrilled with it that he rushes out to take it up stright up to the loft.

At last she holds up a parcel and announces: "Henny, with love from Nan." I open it as fast as I can. It is a pale brown jumper with a pattern in coloured wools around the neck. I hug Nan and she explains that it is a Fair Isle jersey but it doesn't have as many coloured patterns in it as it should have because in Wartime she can't get all the different coloured wools. There is also a pair of navy blue knitted mitts in the parcel.

Then Mother calls out, "For Ted, with love from Nan," and hands us a very small parcel. We open it and there is a tiny matching Ted-sized Fair Isle sweater, exactly like mine. We give her another hug and I take Betty's old frock off him and put on his new jumper. He looks much warmer and very handsome and much more like a boy teddy bear.

She has almost finished handing out the presents to everyone when she says, "Now, Henrietta, I have a special present for you from Briggs. He made it for you because you have been such a help with feeding the rabbits. We did not have enough paper to wrap it in, so, close your eyes, and Felicity, please come and help me bring it in from the hall cupboard." I stand in the middle of the floor and wait.

"Open your eyes, dearest." I open them and there is the little bookcase that I have helped Briggs build.

"But, Mother," I cry, "we made that for Janey, not for me. Briggs told me it was her special Christmas present. It's for Janey, not for me." I jump up and down in agitation.

"No, it's for you, Henrietta," she assures me. "Briggs wanted you to help him build it so that is why he told you it was for Janey. Hugo will put it up for you beside your bed and you can keep all your special picture books on it," This was the best surprise I have ever had; what a lovely friend Briggs is.

Felicity receives books from our mother, which she is very pleased with, one of Nan's new hankies from me and a small screwdriver from Hugh. "I have no idea what I can use this for," she laughs, "but I'm sure that I'll need it one day!"

Hugh rushes back into the house and calls us to come and see what he has found but says that we have to see it from the garden side. We put on our thickest outdoor clothes and wellies and troop out of the back door into the garden. The snow glistens in the sunlight. He points to the front door, where, to our astonishment, a dead wild rabbit is tied to the knocker.

"Take the rabbit down, Hugo, and hand me the note." She reads:

"Happy Christmas from the Gypsies"

"What a useful present; we can make delicious rabbit pie with that can't we? How kind of them, maybe it is because you saw to the child's arm, Nan. What a good start to our Christmas.

Hang it up on the hook by the back door and Nan will see to it later, Hugo and then fill the biggest saucepan with snow so that we can melt it on the range and fill the kettle too," she adds. "Back inside the house everyone as quickly as you can, it really is freezing out here."

I show Ted my presents; a drawing of Father Christmas from Mother, a drawing book that Felicity made me out of notepaper that Nan had found in her trunk, a small bag of marbles from Hugh, (but not my bombsey!), a hanky from Lizzybuff, Nan's jersey and of course, the bookcase. What a lovely Christmas!

As a special treat, a friend of Mother's has sent us a goose for our Christmas dinner. Nan puts it in to cook just before breakfast and once the present giving is over, she goes to check on the goose and comes back looking very worried. She tells us that there is fat oozing out of the oven and when we rush into the kitchen we see it oozing all over the hearthrug and onto the brick floor.

"Oh, Nan, whatever can we do?" our mother wails.

"I don't know, Mum, I always knew that a goose had a lot of fat, but I didn't know anything like this would happen. I think the problem is that the pan is not deep enough. Do you remember that one we had that the government requisitioned? That would have been deep enough."

"Yes, Nan, but I had to give up some pots and pans to them and I had no idea that one day we would have to cook a huge goose! Hugo, go and fill a coalscuttle with ash from the shed," she orders. He returns and she tells him to pour the ash over the greasy floor. "Now, slowly pull the rug away from the stove. Nan, let's stand on the dry piece where the rug was, open the oven door and take the bird out. Stand back, everyone." Nan says that it is far too heavy for Mum to lift and asks Felicity to help.

"Let me," Hugh cries, "I'm the strong Man of the Family." He and Nan struggle and finally get the pan out of the oven and onto the floor.

'We will let the bird cool before we take it out of the pan."

"What can we do with it once it's cooled?" Nan asks.

"I don't know because it is much too fatty to give to the animals; we will have to bury it. What an awful waste of food but I can't think of what else we can do with it."

Felicity helps clean up all the dreadful mess and Nan tells us that when the vegetables are cooked she will scramble some powdered egg and then we can have the Christmas cake for pudding. We sit and eat our meagre Christmas meal with the poor half-cooked goose watching us.

Chapter 21
Hugh's Treasure

One afternoon Hugh bursts into the kitchen carrying a very big untidy bundle in his arms.

"Slow down, Hugo, you nearly knocked me over," Mother snaps. "Whatever have you got there? What is it, and where did you find it?"

"It's a very frosty parachute," Hugh proclaims proudly, full of self-importance. "I found it up on the Downs, up near the Chalky Hills. It was lying in the bottom of a trench. I cut the ropes off the harness, and yes," he adds, before she can ask, "I brought all the pieces of rope home and hung them up in the tool shed." He smiles at us all and, stroking the silky fabric, casually remarks, "It's nice, isn't it?"

"Nice?" questions Mother, "It's not nice, Hugo..." His face falls and he looks as though he thinks he might be in big trouble, "it's *marvellous*! It is real treasure. Look at it, Nan. It isn't silk, it is too bulky. I do believe it is nylon. I wonder if it is German or American? If it was American, I suppose the parachutist would have packed it up and taken it with him, so it must be an enemy one. I did not know there were any parachutes that were not made of silk. Yes," she smiles at me, "the ones you and Ted used to watch at our last house were made of silk and that is why they were such amazing colours. Silk takes dye so perfectly."

"Well," she continues, "fancy finding such a treasure so close to home! Look!" she exclaims, shaking the parachute out all over the table, "there are yards and yards of material, and what an unusual colour too. Is it sea green, or eau-de-nil?"

"I don't know, Mum," replies Nan, who is not artistic.

"I know! I know!" I jump up and down with excitement, "it's turkwoz, that's what colour it is, isn't it?"

"Yes, dear child, you are right, it is turquoise, how clever of you to remember such a difficult name."

"How do you think I should wash it, Mum? It's awfully muddy."

"I have never seen nylon material like this before only those American nylon stockings. I expect you should wash it in cold

107

water, what do you think?"

They discuss this matter further and then she says, "I will make a marvellous full length ball gown for Felicity as a surprise for her sixteenth birthday if the War is over by then. I'll design it especially for her with short puff sleeves, narrow shoulder straps and then make the skirt really full; not only will it look beautiful but it will be a joy to dance in. Just imagine having this amount of fabric to work with after all the years of clothing coupons and short skirts and making do! We will give a dance for her in the drawing room and invite the Vicar's sons and all sorts of young people," she adds vaguely. "Felicity will look superb in this colour with her dark hair."

"Now, everyone, I want to keep this a secret from her, so do not say a word to her from any of you. Do you understand, Hugo? I am very pleased with you for finding it, although I have warned you over and over again about the danger of unexploded shells going off in the trenches, however, I will not say any more about that for now. I will give you an extra sixpence pocket money and a special box that I have been keeping for you for your coin collection as a reward. I want the gown to be a complete surprise for her on the morning of her birthday and if you let the cat out of the bag, young man, I will take the box back immediately."

"Come on, Nan, if you can wash it whilst she is out and hang it in the copper house to dry, we will fold it up and put it in an old pillowcase and hide it at the bottom of the summer trunk until it is time to make the gown."

We have our tea and the Grown Ups continue to discuss the amazing find and Hugh basks in their approval. Mother is in such a good mood that I ask her to tell me the story about the time she sailed in a big ship. We sit in front of the kitchen fire and she begins the proper way.

"Once upon a time there was a beautiful young bride who was going on a long journey to meet her new husband."

"That was you, wasn't it?"

"Yes, of course it was me, now be quiet and listen! I was very nervous, travelling on my own all the way to Egypt. However, I enjoyed the sea journey very much and met several other young officers' wives who were destined for different parts of Africa. When the ship finally docked a young officer came on board to meet me and to escort me to the train. My luggage, including what is now our summer trunk, my hatboxes and my new leather suitcases with my initials embossed in gold on them, were loaded into the guard's van by bearers. The young man settled me into one of the Ladies Only carriages and before the train left two other ladies joined me, also bound for Khartoum in the Sudan. They were pleasant and told me about their lives in that city. One was the wife of a banker and the other of the Police Chief. They told me that we would have to change trains more than once and when we reached Khartoum I would have to travel on my own for the rest of my journey.

"The train whistled and chugged out of the station. Gathering speed it soon left the sun baked buildings of the city behind. I gazed out of the window at the shifting sand and occasionally saw a string of camels and their black-clad handlers crossing the trackless desert.

"Sometimes we passed vivid green oases, like miniature Gardens of Eden, full of date palms and well built houses. One of the ladies explained that each oasis had a caravanserai - a lodging place like an inn where the traders slept and where their camels were rested and watered. In between the oases there were endless miles of desert. As the sun began to set deep shadows emphasized the ripples in the sand dunes.

"I was becoming quite excited because I would soon see my Beloved again. Yes," she sighs, and before I could ask she adds, "your father. I had seen him every day for a month from the day we met until the day we became engaged and then for a week before the wedding two years later. We had our glorious three-month honeymoon and then he returned to Africa. And there I was, months and months later, a new bride of twenty-one, miles and miles from home and everything that I knew, travelling through the star-filled night to meet him once more. What would my new home, and my new life, be like, I wondered.

"I fell asleep in my bunk in the sleeper car listening to the rhythm of the wheels going clackety clack, clackety clack on the track." She looks up and seems surprised to see that she is no longer on the train.

"What happened next? Tell me about the locust going down the front of your frock."

"No, child, that was a most embarrassing event that I would far rather forget. It was just very fortunate that there were only ladies in the carriage. Now sit up at the table and finish your drawing."

The next day I am busy dressing Ted for his birthday party in his Christmas jersey and his blue trousers when my mother sweeps into the Nursery and declares, with excitement ringing in her voice, "Henrietta, I have something I want to tell you about!"

I sit Ted down on the nursing chair and look up at her and enquire, "What is it, Mother?"

"Come here," she says, as she lowers her plump self into a wicker armchair. "Come here and stand beside me." She puts her arm around me and pulls me close.

"Now, where was I? Oh yes, I remember. How would you," she pauses, "like," she pauses yet again, "to have a new baby brother or sister?" She beams expectantly at me.

"No, thank you, we have a baby – Lizzybuff," I reply politely, wriggling out of her embrace. Quite certain that I do not want another baby in the house, I add, "and we don't need another one." She looks really shocked so I quickly change the subject. "Just look at Ted, Mother! Doesn't he look sweet all dressed up for his birthday party?"

After tea I was helping Nan wash up when she said to me, "You know, Henny, your mother was not at all happy when you said you didn't want a new brother or sister. Babies are so sweet; wouldn't you like to have one to play with?"

"No thank you, Nan, we have one. Lizzybuff is our baby. We don't need another." I carefully dry my silver mug with the teacloth, breathe on it and give it a good polish, "Ted says he had a very nice party. Even Clementina brought him a present - a sweet little mouse. I knew you wouldn't like it if we kept it in the nursery because it was dead so I told her to take it out and she did."

"Let's finish the drying up and then go up to bed and I'll

read to you. Come along, you both must be very tired after the party. Which book shall I read?"

"Please read me *Miranda Mouse.*" She agrees, and I skip along the landing, the idea of another baby quite forgotten.

The next morning Mother comes into the kitchen, frowns at me and says that she is going to write a letter to the Colonel telling him about a certain young lady not wanting another brother or sister. She goes into the drawing room to write at her desk still looking upset.

Chapter 22
The Gift of a Melon

Nan says that spring is nearly here and I ask her if we can go to Tilsham this afternoon so that I can walk through Fairyland but she says no, we are going to Chittingford and posting Mother's letter on the way. I ask her if I can stop to pick snowdrops in the Vicarage garden and she says yes, but that I will have to be the one to ask the Vicar for permission.

When we reach the Vicarage we stop and she opens the side gate for me. I bravely walk up the long driveway to the front door of the Vicarage and, standing on tiptoe, ring the bell. I wait for ages and then the door opens so suddenly that I nearly fall backwards down the steps. The Vicar looks very tall and scary in his long black frock.

"Yes, young lady, and what can I do for you?" he asks rather sternly.

I look up at him as he towers above me and explain that I am the Colonel's daughter from Upper Nettlebourne and I would like to pick some of his snowdrops.

"Well," he replies, with what might be a twinkle in his eye, "if you are the Colonel's daughter, then I must allow you to pick as many as you want, mustn't I? Is that your Nanny waiting for you at the gate?"

"Yes, and my baby sister, Lizzybuff."

"Well hurry up and don't keep them waiting too long because the afternoon is drawing in and it is getting colder as we speak."

I thank him and walk back down the drive stopping here and there to pick the flowers until I have a large bunch. I hand them to Nan who puts them in the pram and then we walk home as fast as we can. I arrange them in a vase and place it on the supper table as a surprise for Mother.

On our way home Nan tells me that someone called Nurse Pomfrey will arrive tomorrow to look after Mother for a few days. She explains that Nurse Pomfrey had trained her to be a nanny when she was young.

"Why is she coming? Is Mother ill?"

"No, she is just a bit tired and she needs to be looked after."

"Why can't you look after her, Nan?"

"Because I'm too busy looking after you and Lizzybuff, doing the cooking, the washing and everything else and I am much too busy to answer any more of your endless questions."

We arrive home and after tea Nan asks me to help her tidy up the nursery before bedtime.

Nurse Pomfrey arrives on the before-lunch bus. We meet her at the gate. She is tall and thin and dressed in a navy blue coat with matching hat and gloves and black stockings and shoes. and she is carrying a large black bag. Her white hair is pulled tightly back into a bun and she looks very old and very frightening.

She shakes hands with Nanny, who says that she hopes that she had had a good journey. "Least said, soonest mended," she replies sourly.

I wonder what got broken but am far too scared to ask.

Nan then introduces me. "Nurse Pomfrey, this is Henrietta." I smile up at her and she puts out her hand for me to shake.

"I trust that you are a well behaved child," she barks. "At a time like this I have no truck with naughty, demanding children who ask questions all the time." Nan hastens to assure her that I am a model child with perfect manners and that I never ask questions.

"Humph," she snorts, "time will tell, that is what I always say, Nanny, time will tell. Please show me to my room." We take her up to Felicity's room, which has been turned into a temporary guest room. Felicity has gone to spend the day with a school friend in Patisford and will sleep in the smaller spare room for the three nights that Nurse will stay with us.

Nurse removes her coat and hat and I see that she is dressed in a navy blue uniform frock with the same sort of starched collars and cuffs that Nan wears in the afternoon. She opens her black bag and takes out her apron and a white headdress and puts them on. This makes her look even scarier. "Nanny, please take me straight to Mrs. Rowansforde so that I can assess the situation," she demands.

Nan suggests that I take the vegetable scraps out to the barn for the rabbits whilst she takes Nurse Pomfrey to meet my mother, who, for some strange reason, is still in bed. I go to feed the rabbits and have a chat with Briggs, who is making a special nest for Norah, in one of the bigger

cages. As I am telling him all about Nurse arriving, Nan calls me in for lunch so I say goodbye to him and to all the rabbits and run back to the house.

Nurse Pomfrey sits at the lunch table as stiff as a board. Nan serves her first, then me and then Lizzybuff, who shouts, "No like, Nanny! No like!" Leaning over the side of her highchair she throws her silver dish onto the ground spilling her lunch all over the floor. Giggling and throwing her messy hands up in the air she joyfully exclaims "Oooh!"

Nurse Pomfrey looks horrified at such behaviour. "She doesn't like carrots," Nan says apologetically, "How silly of me, I shouldn't have given her any."

"Carrots are good for the eyesight," pronounces the Nurse. Nan hastily mops up the mess on the floor and gives Lizzybuff a rusk to eat instead. Lunch continues in silence.

"When do you think . . . ?" Nanny begins.

"Tomorrow morning," replies Nurse Pomfrey.

"What's tomorrow morning," I ask curiously, feeling that they are hiding something from me.

"Never you mind, young lady," she snaps. "Just eat up and do not interrupt when Grown-Ups are talking." I sit miserably at the table, trying not to ask questions, which is always very hard.

After a long silence, Nurse Pomfrey announces, "I brought a melon with me for dessert as a gift," she says, giving me a frosty smile.

Nan slices and serves the melon and then Nurse takes out a small glass bottle and sprinkles brown powder onto each slice.

"Cinnamon," she declares, "pre-War cinnamon. Melon does not taste right without it."

I take one bite. It tastes musty and disgusting and I spit it out onto my plate. Nurse Pomfrey gasps and, rising from her seat, looks as though she is going to box my ears.

"I am so sorry, Nurse," Nan says hurriedly, "that was very naughty, Henrietta. Whatever has got into you today? Now come along, I'll put you in the nursery and deal with you later," she says severely. We leave the table and, once safe in the nursery, she gives me a big hug.

"Nan, it was disgusting," I say, pulling away from her and making a terrible face.

"I know," she agrees, beginning to laugh. "It was disgusting, but you shouldn't have said so, you really made Nurse very cross. Oh dear!" she chuckles, "the look on her face when you spat it out!" She laughs even harder and then, pulling herself together, she tells me to relax in the big chair with dear Ted and she promises that once Nurse has returned upstairs she will bring me something special to eat.

Chapter 23
Charlotte's Arrival

The next morning, on my way to have breakfast, I hear a piecing scream coming from upstairs.

"What's that, Nan? Is that my mother screaming?"

"No, Henny, of course it isn't."

"It is, Nan, I'm going to see," I start up the stairs. "I think she's hurt."

"No, Henrietta, come here at once," she orders, grabbing my hand. "I have a real treat for you and I will tell you all about it, but please go and feed the rabbits first, they must be very hungry. Then come back and sit quietly whilst I make our breakfast.

I hurry off and do what I am told because I am so worried it doesn't occur to me not to obey her. Anyway, I usually do what Nan tells me to because I don't like her getting into trouble with my mother. When I return I can hear more noises from upstairs, not screams this time, but what sound more like moans.

"What is that Nurse doing to her? I don't like her and I think she's hurting Mother and I wish she hadn't come," I whimper.

Nan ignores my comments and asks, "Don't you want to know what the treat is?"

"Yes, please." I pick up Ted, who is busy relaxing on the counter, and climb up onto a chair and sit with him clutched in my arms. Nan closes the door and sits down on the chair beside us.

"Now," she begins, "your very special treat is…" before she can finish I interrupt her, "I know what it is, Nan! You've got a new tin of broken biscuits from the shop! Can I have all the jammy bits?"

"No, that is not what it is, although now you mention it, it would be a good idea to buy another tin as we've finished the last one. I'll have to ask Mr. Collins if he has any. Now, stop interrupting and let me tell you about your treat, and this is a really big one."

"After breakfast you are going to Patisford on the bus with Briggs. He is getting some rabbits ready to take with you to sell and he says he will spend time showing you the animals in the

Market and in the Cattle Market. Then you can help him do some shopping for us. I will pack sandwiches and you can eat them in the Abbey gardens and then catch the bus home in time for tea."

"Thank you Nanny. Yes, that is a very nice treat; I've never been on the bus with Briggs. Can I have sugar sandwiches?"

"No, Henny, of course you can't. You know we've run out of sugar and Granny hasn't sent us any recently."

"Can I wear my new Christmas jumper you knitted me? Can Ted come? Which rabbits are we taking? Oh, dear! What happens if I want to go to the lavatory because Briggs can't take me, can he, he's a man?"

Nanny ignores most of my questions, as she usually does, because she says that so many questions at once make her head spin. However, she does answer the really important one. "Just whisper to Briggs if you need to 'go' and he will take you to the Victory Restaurant and ask one of the waitresses to take you to the bathroom. That's what he does if his Janey wants to 'go'. So don't you worry, Briggs and I discussed that already. And I don't expect you'll have to 'go' anyway." Nan has trained me to last all day when we are out because she does not approve of public lavatories, because of germs, or of going in the hedge if we are on a walk, because that is rude.

Briggs arrives dressed in his uniform, carrying the boxes with the rabbits inside. He smiles at me and assures me that he has remembered to put the rabbits' breakfasts in with them.

"Can Ted come with us, please Briggs, he'll be very quiet."

"Better not, Henny," Briggs replies, "it's still a bit cold out for teddy bears you know, you don't want him to get bronchitis do you?" I picture poor Ted in bed, coughing his head off and Nan giving him M & B to make him better, so I agree to leave him at home in the warm nursery.

"You must hold Briggs' hand once you get off the bus, mustn't she Briggs?"

"Of course, Nanny. Janey always holds me hand when we go shopping in Patisford. Now let's go out to the street or we'll miss the bus. You climb on first and then run as fast as you can up the stairs and climb up onto the front seat before it starts off again. The rabbits and I will be following right behind."

Once we are well on our journey and have gone over the bump, I confide in Briggs that I heard my mother scream and I am very worried about her.

"Oh, no, Henny, your mother wouldn't scream. Ladies like your mother don't ever scream. It must have been the old screech owl that lives at the Dairy Farm that you heard. He's been around a lot lately, even in the daytime."

I am just about to ask him why the horrid Nurse is at our house and why Mother is still in bed, when he tells me that we need lots more names for the babies that Heather has produced the night before. "We need five names, Henny. Hold out your hand." I did so. "You have to find this many names, one for each finger, and one for your thumb, all girls' names. So, think of some when you go to bed tonight and then tell me tomorrow. The new babies also mean," he continues, "that we will need to make more cages and we have no chicken wire left because we have used up all that roll that you and Hugh found in the walled garden. However, I hear that the Vicar has an old chicken run he doesn't use, maybe Hugh could ask him for the wire?"

"The Vicar doesn't like Hugh, Briggs, and I know that Hugh hates him, so maybe Mother could ask him? He likes her."

"Maybe when she is not so busy," he replies. Looking out of the window he exclaims, "Just look at all those wild rabbits in that field! Just think, if we made each one into a rabbit pie, how many pies we would have!" I don't like the idea of any rabbits being killed, but we have to eat whatever we can get in Wartime and rabbit pie is delicious. And, after all, I reason, wild rabbits don't count as real rabbits like Jilly, Snowball, Freddy, Paisley and Sophia and all my other special pet ones.

The bus arrives in town and we head for the Market. Our rabbits are quickly sold and I bid a tearful goodbye to Johnny, Belinda, Letty and Jack. Briggs mops my eyes with his big khaki handkerchief and assures me that they are all going to good homes. Taking my hand, we pass all the other rabbits in the rows of cages; they press their dear little noses against the wire and waffle them at me. I love every one of them and I wish we could buy them all and take them home together with ours that have just sold.

We make our way into the Cattle Market and spend time there looking at the cows and at the big brown bull, who huffs and puffs and stamps his feet and looks very frightening. Briggs assures me that he cannot get out of his pen. I wish I had not seen him because I know he will give me nightmares. "Let's go, Briggs, I don't like the bull. Can we go and see the sheep, please?"

After we have a good look at the sheep and their lambs, we go and do some shopping for Mother and then buy a few things Nan needs, including some new nappy pins. Then it is time to go to the Abbey Gardens to eat our sandwiches. We sit on a bench in the pale sunlight and watched the people going into the Abbey to pray. The sound of organ music floats across the unkempt lawns "I wish Janey had come with us, Briggs, please can she come and play with me one day?"

"We'll have to see about that, Henny. You know that your mother doesn't like having other children to play, because she says she already has enough of her own. Now, have you had enough to eat? Help me pack up the things back into the basket and let's get going again." He lowers his voice, "Do you need to...?"

"No, thank you Briggs, I don't; I can wait until we get home."

As we pass through the fruit and vegetable market in the Square on the way to the bus I ask him if we can buy a little bunch of violets for Mother. I hand him my purse and he counts out the money into the flower lady's hand. I carry them carefully all the way home.

Nanny meets us at the gate looking very excited. "All well, Nanny?" Briggs enquires, raising his eyebrows at her. She nods and smiles at him. "Henny was very well behaved and we had a good time, didn't we?" I thank him and ask Nan if Ted has been good.

"Very good indeed; he was no trouble at all. Thank you Briggs for giving her such a happy time and for doing all the shopping." She smiles at him as he hands her the shopping basket. He says that he has to go and put the rabbits to bed before he goes home.

"Look at what I bought Mother with my very own money, Nan!" I wave the little bunch of flowers in the air as Nan takes off my coat.

"She'll love those, that was very sweet of you and she has a very special surprise for you too. Bring the flowers with you and we will go upstairs so that she can show you what it is." We climb the stairs hand in hand; Nan knocks and then opens the bedroom door.

Mother is sitting up in bed wearing the new pale pink lacy bed jacket that Nan has just finished knitting for her. In her arms is a bundle. "Look, dearest," she says as she pulls the shawl back and, there, to my dismay, is a very small, very pink, baby human, which opens its mouth and gives a squeal. I jump back in alarm and drop the flowers. "Come here, Henrietta, this is your new baby sister," she announces.

Nan looks lovingly at the baby, her eyes sparkling with excitement, "Isn't she lovely, darling?" she asks me.

"No, Nan," I burst out, "she's very ugly and we don't need another baby, we've got Lizzybuff. I told you that before. Can't Nurse put her back in her big bag and take her away again?" I beg, tears beginning to well up inside me. I swallow hard because I don't want to cry in front of the horrid Nurse who has caused all this trouble. "Please," I add, hoping that the magic word will make a difference.

"Humph!" says Nurse Pomfrey, "that child needs a good beating, Nanny. Spare the rod, you know. What a bad-mannered child," she frowns nastily at me. I hide behind Nan's skirt.

Mother sighs dramatically and murmurs, "Take her away, Nanny, I am tired," and, closing her eyes, she cuddles the new baby closer to her and turns her head away.

As we go downstairs Nan shakes her head and says that I have upset my mother badly and that I should be very pleased to have another sister. I tell her that I am badly upset too and that I would much rather have a puppy than another baby. "Oh! I didn't give her my flowers," I cry, suddenly remembering that I had dropped them beside the bed, "please, will you go back and give them to her?" She assures me that she will next time she goes upstairs, meanwhile, she suggests that I go and have a chat with my goat friend.

I run down the garden and as I squeeze around the elm tree into the next-door garden, I notice how full the river is. Maybe Hugh will help me try to catch some fish? I look up and there, waiting patiently for me is 'Gustus. I tell him about everything that has happened, the horrid Nurse, the disgusting melon and the awful new baby human. As always, he looks more amused than concerned by my tales of woe and is not much comfort. Oh well! He is only a goat, even if he is a very handsome one. I say goodbye without even stopping to brush him because I still feel sort of bumpy inside and my tummy aches. I return slowly to the house.

Just wait until Hugh comes home from school and finds out that we have another baby sister. He will be very upset too. It's all that nasty Nurse's fault.

After supper Nan takes Lizzybuff and me up to bed and I soon fall fast asleep after such an exciting and upsetting day. I am dreaming of sheep and lambs, of rabbits crying, of catching fish with nappy pins and of being chased into the dirty river by a huge brown bull when Nan wakes me up.

"Henny, are you all right? Crying out so loudly like that, you nearly woke Elizabeth! If you ask me, you've had too much excitement for one day. Were you having bad dreams?" I nod. "Hush, now, everything is all right, you're quite safe. I'll sit here beside you until you go back to sleep."

"Please tell me a story, Nan."

"I'm not as good at telling stories as your mother, but I will try. Once upon a time," I sigh with contentment because she is starting the story in the proper way, "a long time ago there were three very naughty...." Seeing that I have already dropped off to sleep she tucks me in and tiptoes out of the night nursery.

Chapter 24
The Train Wreck

Hugh spent a lot of time up in the barn loft during the first few weeks at The Old Manor Farmhouse laying out his train set. Since then he has added all sorts of different things including the new tunnel he received for Christmas. The tracks now snake across a large area of the loft floor in great big loopy patterns and he has a regiment of lead soldiers lined up on one of the platforms. There are porters, signals and tiny trolleys laden with miniature luggage. In the middle of the tracks there is a farm, a farmhouse, some small barns and a pond, which he made using an old mirror Mother gave him. There are horses, sheep and pigs and even some tiny piglets arranged in the fenced in fields. The painted lead haystack is surounded by several flat trees that look very odd but Hugh doesn't seem to mind.

Overhead his model planes hang from the rafters on black thread. They look as though they really are flying through the gloomy loft. When he is playing with his train set he props the door open to let light in.

He tells me that I may come up into the loft this afternoon to watch the trains if I behave myself. I invite Clementina to come too and she sits on one side of me and Ted leans against me on the other. Hugh turns on the switch and the trains start whizzing around the track. Clementina gives a start but I put my arm around her to remind her not to chase them. She really does know that she must not touch and she smiles up at me as if to assure me that she too is on her best behaviour. We sit and watch, entranced by the tiny railway. My mind begins to wander and I am trying to decide which story I will ask Mother to tell me this evening. Maybe, the one about the time that she and our father....

Suddenly there is pandemonium. Whilst I am day-dreaming, Clementina has lost patience and pounced on one of the trains and both the engine and most of the carriages crash and lie in a tangled heap beside the lines. The entire regiment of soldiers lie dead on the tracks, all the trolleys are turned upside down, the lampposts have toppled over and the animals are scatered all over the floor.

"Get out!" screams my brother, his face scarlet with rage. "Get out! You and that damn fat cat and that stupid teddy bear, get out or I will throw you all out of the door down into the stinging nettles."

Clementina flees, leaving Ted and me to cope. Stupidly, I retort, "You said a bad word! I'll tell Mother!"

"Don't you dare," he roars, moving closer to me. Now I am really scared and my heart begins to jump up and down so much I really think that it will fall out of the bottom of my cardigan. "If you tell," he continues in a menacing voice, "I'll hang you and that damn cat, and that damn Ted upside down in the Ghosty Hole until your eyes all fall out!" I burst into tears and feel sick.

He begins to reset the trains, then looks up and snarls, "What are you waiting for, Henrietta?" Hugh never calls me anything but Henny, so I know that I am in big trouble.

"I can't get down by myself," I snivel.

"Then, how did you get up here?" he demands.

"I tucked Ted into the top of my skirt, then climbed up into the manger, stood on the edge of it, climbed up on top of a rabbit hutch and then sort of pulled us through the hay rack and up through the gap."

"If you can get up, you can get down," he reasons.

That is simply not true. I have always been very good at climbing up, but very bad at climbing down again. However, Ted and I finally do manage to get down with a bit of help from Hugh, and sobbing and hiccupping, I run back to the house where Nan is in the kitchen making lunch.

"Whatever is the matter with you?" she asks kindly. Wiping her hands on her apron, she sits down on a chair. "You and Ted are very dusty, wherever have you been? Come here and tell your dear old Nanny what happened."

"Nothing," I fib, "I just got a bit frightened getting down from the loft."

"I think that there is more to it than that," she says shaking her head, "I suspect that Hugh has been up to some sort of funny business," she adds knowingly, but did not say any more. My dear Nan, she always knows when not to ask too many questions.

"I've just finished making the cottage pie so climb up on the stool here and take this fork and you can scratch wavy patterns into the mashed potato, I know how much you like doing that."

I finish drawing on the pie and then, gathering Ted up in my arms, I climb up onto the windowsill to think about what has happened. We decide that we will not go and watch the trains again until we are both much, much bigger and that, next time, we will not invite Clementina to join us.

A tall stranger passes the window. "Who is that man, Nan?" She comes over to the window to look.

"I think that he's a Prisoner of War, Henny, probably from that prison camp past Tilsham."

As he turns I notice there was a big dark red patch on the back of his overalls and I ask what it is.

"That," she replies, in a no-nonsense voice, "that patch," she pauses, "is where you shoot them if they give you any trouble. Right between the shoulder blades," she adds.

"But, Nan, we don't have a gun!"

"Of course we don't! What I mean is that that is where the army would shoot him if they had to."

"Why would they have to, Nan?"

"Because! Now stop asking questions and come and help me get the washing off the line."

Later that evening Mother agrees to continue the story if I sit very quietly and don't interrupt.

"We arrived in Khartoum and I was met by an officer and his wife and taken to a very grand hotel where we had dinner and I stayed the night. The next morning I boarded the train for my new home, which was another four hundred miles further into the desert. Every mile was a mile nearer to my husband and a mile further from England."

"Eventually the train chuffed into the station and there was your father waiting to meet me. It was many months since I had seen him because he left England straight after our honeymoon. He looked so tanned and handsome standing there on the platform in his tropical uniform."

"We shook hands and he kissed my cheek. Then we were driven along a track in the desert to our new quarter in the military camp. The cook, his batman and all the other staff were lined up on the front path to welcome me. Your father introduced me to them and then showed me around the house. He whispered discreetly that the lavatory was in the garden and the maid would show me where it was later on but that I had to be very careful and watch out for scorpions when I went out there. The gardener had laid rows of pebbles on either side of the path to the lavatory and painted them white, especially for me. He told me that the shower was a bucket filled with water that had been heated by the sun and he explained that when I pulled the rope the water would cascade over me. It was all so different from England - and so very hot. However, by the time the sun had set the temperature dropped dramatically and I was glad that I had brought several warm shawls with me."

She pauses, a dreamy smile on her face, and I can see that she is remembering those long ago days. I wait as patiently as I can and then ask her to tell me about the polo ponies.

"No, dear child, I'll tell you about them another time. It is getting late. Run along and ask Nanny to put you to bed."

Chapter 25
A Time for Dyeing

Nan puts our new baby, Charlotte, in the pram and wheels it into the shade of the elderberry tree, which is laden with whitish blossom. I hate this tree when it has flowers, because they smell disgusting, give me a headache and make me sneeze. The days are getting warmer and sunnier so Briggs has taken off the grey pram hood this morning and replaced it with the cream-coloured green-lined canopy, which has a long fringes all the way round, which wobble when the pram moves.

I am getting used to Charlotte who, Nan says, with her golden curls, looks like a cherub. The best thing about her is that she sleeps most of the time, so I don't have much to do with her and she does not take up too much of Nan's attention. Because cats love the warm, milky smell of a baby Nan is afraid that one might jump up into the pram and suffocate Charlotte. This is why she always fastens the cat net over the pram when the baby is in it.

"Clementina wouldn't do that, she told me she doesn't even like baby humans."

"What nonsense are you on about now, Henny?" Nanny asks. "Animals don't like or dislike people."

"Oh yes, they do, Nanny," I assure her earnestly, "Poor Old Bunker does not like me a bit and I don't like him either, he is a very boring old dog, and," I pause, knowing I am taking a big risk, add, "he stinks." (Stink is considered a very bad word in our house).

Luckily, Nanny ignores my last remark and asks, curiously, "How do you know he doesn't like you?"

"Clementina told me," I reply.

"Well, whatever next? I don't have time to talk about such silliness. It's a nice, sunny day and we have lots to do. Come and help me fire up the copper so that I can do some washing."

"Can Ted come, Nanny? He promises to be very good."

"Better not, Henny, he might get washed by mistake. Leave him in the kitchen. He can wait there for us." I sit him in the highchair and wave goodbye.

When Briggs arrived one of the first jobs he did was to scrub out the copper house, distemper the walls and he even found an old piece of linoleum to put down on the floor to make it nicer for Nan to do the washing in.

The kindling box is empty, so I collect some from the tool shed. She kneels on the floor on her canvas-covered kneeler and lays the fire with newspaper and some of the kindling.

"Now we have to fill the copper. Bring that empty bucket and we'll fill it at the tap in the yard." She struggles back and forth several times with buckets of cold water pouring each one in until it is full enough. Putting the big round lid on she says it is time to light the fire. "Run into the kitchen, please, and bring me another box of matches, this one is empty."

I return with the matches and ask if I can light the fire. "Of course not! You are much too young to use matches. Hand me the box and move away a bit, I don't want you to get burnt."

"Like poor Shirley?

Nanny sits back on her heels looking astonished. "My goodness me, how ever do you know about that!"

"I heard Mr. Collins telling someone in the shop,"

"For someone with such tiny ears, you do hear an awful lot of things that you shouldn't, I must say. That poor Shirley, it's a very sad story but it does show just how careful we all have to be with fire."

What I overheard was, that Shirley, who was seven years old and lived across the road from us, was ill in bed last winter with bronchitis. To keep her warm in the bitterly cold weather, her mother lit the fire in her bedroom fireplace. One evening, Shirley got out of bed, climbed up a chair to get a book off the mantelpiece, lost her balance, fell into the hearth and her nightie caught fire. She was burned to death.

Nan knows that I am still worrying about it, so, to take my mind off the tragic tale, she asks me to run and ask Mother if she has anything that she would like to have washed. "It is such a windy day I can get lots of things dry in no time."

I search the house for her and finally find her sitting in the drawing room in one of the big armchairs. She smiles happily at me and tells me that our father has written to say that he had just returned safely from a long trek into the mountain district. A terrible sandstorm had blown up and it had taken him and his men an extra week to reach back to camp. "Reading about it makes me feel as though there is sand in my clothes. Those storms were terrible. The sand got in everywhere, even up my nose, although I kept it tightly covered."

She shook off her memories and returns to our world. "Now where was I?" she asks. "Ah, yes," she smiles, "what are you and Nan up to, and where are the two Little Ones?"

"Charlotte is fast asleep in the pram under the smelly tree, and Lizzybuff is playing in the playpen in the nursery chatting to herself in gobbledegook; I think she's making up stories. Nanny has just lit the copper and wants to know if you have anything special to be washed?"

"Let me think about that," she replies, "but first of all, come out into the garden with me, Henrietta, dearest, it is such a beautiful sunny morning." We look at the flowers and then at the vegetable patch and she points out how the plants all grow in rows. "I want you to learn to really look at things, Henrietta, and to remember them; what colour they are, where the shadows fall and what you like about them. Then later on you can draw them from memory." I listen carefully, pleased that we are talking about what she calls art. She is always so happy when she receives a letter and I know that she misses her Beloved very much indeed. I don't, because I have never met him.

"Just look at the colour of the sky, it's so very blue," she continues, "that colour blue is called azure. It is the colour of the sky in Africa, except when there is a sandstorm and then everything goes dark. Look, there are no clouds at all, so maybe we will have good weather like this for our birthdays, darling. Next month we will celebrate them with a birthday tea between us. I know what we will do today," she suddenly exclaims in an excited voice, "come on follow me!"

We hurry back into the house and, as we rush from room to room, she collects up some of our bedspreads, the nursery curtains, my best frilly blouse, her old apron, a pair of discoloured white socks and some hankies. "I have a packet of something special in my desk," she exclaims, as she hurries off to the drawing room and returns waving a packet of dye. "Look," she cries, "It is exactly the right colour, azure blue. How lucky! Now come on, child, let's go and tell Nanny what we are going to do."

We go out of the back door into the yard and then into the copper house where Nan is sorting the washing. The water in the copper is beginning to boil. "I'm just going to wash the nappies first and then I have some other clothes. Whatever have you got there, Mum?" she asks, looking at the big bundle of things in her arms.

"Nan it is such a lovely day and I have a packet of dye and so I thought I would like to dye all these things blue, azure blue," she adds.

Nanny looks puzzled. "Why?" she asks, "why ever do you want to dye them blue?"

"To match the sky, of course! Nan, just come outside and look at the sky, just look at it, it is pure azure blue. Come on, be a good sport, I'll wash out the copper for you afterwards and then you can do your other washing."

"Did you have a letter from the Colonel?" Nan enquires.

"I did, Nan darling, I did!" she exclaims, "and I really do want to dye these clothes." She pours in the dye and stirs it with a clean stick that I fetched from the tool shed. Then she adds in each of the items and stirs them. "Now," she says, looking around the copper house, "what else can we put in?" I think that she has her eye on 'Nanny's flags'. Nan thinks so too, because she says, sternly:

"No, Mum, you are not going to dye any of my baby's nappies," she pauses, "azure blue, or," she adds, "any other colour!"

Mother manages to look astonished, although I knew she had thought that nappies would look much more interesting bright blue. "It never crossed my mind, Nan," she replies innocently and winks at me when Nan has her back to us. I giggle and think that this is quite the best day we have had for ages. I love it when she is so happy. Some days she is so sad that she stays up in her bedroom or shuts herself in the drawing room and we hardly ever see her.

"We forgot to put any salt in the water, do you think they

will be colour-fast?"

"Yes, I am sure they will. The problem is that the dye will probably come off on my clothes pegs…"

"I will boil them in clean water afterwards and they will be fine," she assures her. "Now, stand back, Henrietta, whilst I take the things out with the tongs and put them in the buckets. Then we will rinse them in cold water in the scullery sink, mangle them and hang them out to dry. It won't hold you up, Nan, they will dry very fast." Nanny is not too happy about putting them through the old cast-iron mangle in case the dye comes off on the rubber rollers, which are beginning to wear out but my mother soon jollies her along and says that, when we have finished, we will have a very special treat for elevenses and that, once the War is over, she will buy Nan lots and lots of new rubber rollers.

She feeds the dripping cloths through the mangle while Nan turns the handle, sighing and clucking a bit as blue dye pours out into the tub below. My mother smiles at her; she is in such a good mood that Nan can't be cross with her for long.

Poor Old Bunker wanders into the yard from the garden but I shoo him out again because having a blue spotted coat might make him even more miserable. I hand the washing to my mother and she shakes each piece out and pegs it up on the line.

"Look," she exclaims, "it looks as though we have pieces of the sky fluttering in the wind, doesn't it?" she asks me. It certainly is the most unusual line of washing I have ever seen.

"It's the same colour as those tiny butterflies we see up on the Chalky Hills, isn't it, Mummy?"

"Yes, Henrietta, it is; how clever of you to observe that."

We go back into the house and I suddenly notice the palms of my hands. They are blue! I show her and, when we check, hers are too. "Don't say a word," she whispers, "let's go into the kitchen and wait for Nan." She soon joins us, and Mother says, "We have a surprise for you, Nan dear. Close your eyes." She holds up her blue palms and nods at me to do the same and then tells her to open them.

When Nan sees our hands she bursts out laughing and says that at least they match the washing and the sky. She says that she has to check on Elizabeth and Charlotte and then she will make the tea and make up a beaker of National Orange Juice for me. Meanwhile, I tell Ted what has happened and how lucky it was that he had stayed safely in the kitchen or he might have become a blue teddy bear.

"Now, Henrietta," Mother says after we have all washed our hands, "we will work on what I was telling you about shadows. You can draw on this opened envelope. Here's a soft pencil. Draw me a picture of the barn." I draw the barn. "Yes, that's right, a little longer and a bit taller. Now put the roof on, yes, it quite high up, isn't it? What about the doors? Draw them and the stable ones too." I concentrate hard. "Now put in the tree under which Nanny puts Charlotte's pram. That's very good. You are getting to be quite an accomplished artist, Henrietta. Now colour your drawing whilst I embroider my picture."

She puts on her spectacles, threads her needle with green silk and embroiders the lawn in her little picture of a cottage with a garden full of flowers. She draws her own designs on small pieces of clean linen and sometimes I am allowed to help her choose the coloured silks for the picture.

I colour carefully and put in some blue sky and some birds flying overhead. "I've finished," I proclaim, waving my picture in her face.

"Very good! But don't you think that it looks a bit flat? Let us see if we can improve it. Draw the lines of the weatherboarding across the barn very carefully. No! Slow down! Let me show you." She draws straight lines across the barn. "Now you try." I draw in the rest of the boards. "Yes, that's right, but not so fast. You are always in such a hurry! Use the dark brown crayon to darken them and remember to put a dark line under the eaves where the swallows make their nests in the spring. Colour the slate roof dark grey, yes, use the lead pencil. With the ruler add the planks in the doors but this time they go from top to bottom. Good! Now if the sun is coming from the riverside the shadows will be on the other side on the drawing, you will have to darken that side. Now hold it up and see what a difference that makes to the drawing."

"What about the tree? Does it need shadows?"

"Yes, it does. Because you have already coloured it light green you need to add some darker green patches and make the trunk darker brown on that side. See if you can colour the sky a brighter blue..."

"Like the washing?" She laughs and agrees that it should be . . .

"Azure blue," we both chorus.

Chapter 26
The End of the War

The church bells are ringing as I wake up so I know it must be Sunday. I lie in bed and listen to the joyful sound. Mother suddenly rushes in and says that I must get out of bed at once and come downstairs. She says that Nanny is going to make scrambled eggs for a special breakfast treat.

"Why? I ask sleepily. "Is it my birthday? Or is it your birthday?"

"No, dearest, it is not your birthday, or my birthday. Mr. Churchill has just announced on the wireless that it is Victory in Europe Day. VE Day. It is the end of the War!"

"Is our father downstairs? Can I see him? Will he have breakfast with us?"

"No," replies Mother very crossly, and before I can ask any more questions, she repeats, "No, he is not here."

"But you said…"

"I know what I said but the War Office feel differently and he is still away."

"Why? You promised when the War ended he would come home and…."

"Stop it," she shouts in exasperation, sounding as though she is going to cry. "Just get out of bed and come downstairs and stop asking questions." She storms out of the night nursery leaving Ted and me and all the toys feeling very shaken and nervous. Why, if the War is over, is she so cross?

Nan comes into the room and helps me wash and dress. I tell her how cross Mother is. "Will we still have our birthday tea party?" I ask.

"Yes, Henny, of course we can, it'll be one day next week and you may help me make the birthday cake. Good gracious me! You will be five years old!"

"Will I be a Big One then, Nan?"

"Not quite, Henny. Now let's go downstairs and you can help me by laying the table.

At breakfast Mother remarks how lucky it is that we had all the rosettes finished and delivered to Mrs. Gage in time and how quickly they will sell now the War has ended. "Maybe we will receive an order for some more, Nan."

Later in the day, Mr. Collins sends us a message that there will be a Thanksgiving Service for Peace in Europe in the Abbey on Sunday. Mother is very pleased and tells us she plans to attend.

"What a joyful service it will be, Nan! Shall we all go?"

"Why don't you go on your own, Mum? I'll stay here with the family. I think that you will enjoy it more by yourself." She smiles gratefully and goes upstairs to decide what she will wear.

There is a big party at lunchtime and everyone in the village gets together to celebrate. Our neighbours drag tables and chairs out of their houses and bring out food and drink and they all sit down to eat, right in the middle of the village street. Someone plays a violin and they all sing.

Hugh helps me climb up onto the top of the garden wall and we hide under the branches of the tree amongst the ivy and watch the goings on, wishing that we could join in but my mother told us that it was not a party for us but for the village, and so we cannot go.

Once it is dark we watch from our bedroom window as the bonfire is lit. For some reason Hugh is allowed to join in with everyone as they laugh and clap and dance around the fire.

And so the War ends but nothing changes much except that Mother tells Briggs to put the gas masks up into the loft because

we will not need them any more and I am glad about that.

We have our birthday tea in the garden under the smelly tree. Felicity has picked a big punnet of her strawberries especially for us. Nan has decorated the tiny birthday cake with daisies and has placed a stump of candle on it and an old frill around it. Mother tells me to shut my eyes and make a wish when she helps me cut the first slice. I really want a pony, a piano and ginger hair, so I wish for them all. After tea Felicity plays games with us and then I chase Lizzybuff around in circles until she falls down, laughing helplessly.

"My darlings, I have some very exciting news," Mother announces a few days later. "Now the War is over, the American Red Cross is holding a party and you have all been invited."

"I don't have a party frock," Felicity complains.

"I have nearly finished knitting that very grown up green frock for you, I am sure that I can finish it in time…"

"I can't go to a party in a knitted one!"

"I am very sorry Felicity, if, after all the work I have put in, night after night, knitting that frock and ruining my fingers with the rough bouclé wool, it is not good enough for you to wear to the party," Mother says huffily, "then you will have to stay home."

Oh dear! There's going to be a scene.

My sister smiles angelically, "I didn't mean that, Mama. I meant that party frocks are usually shiny and frilly, like all your beautiful evening clothes in the trunk," she adds, diplomatically.

Somewhat mollified, she suggests that we open the summer trunk after tea and see what we can find. As the party is not until Saturday she will have plenty of time to alter a frock to fit Felicity.

"Hugo, you can wear your school uniform with your blazer." Hugh nods, but doesn't say anything. He does not care at all what he wears; it all gets torn and ripped anyway when he gets into a fight. "And," she continues sternly, "don't you get into any trouble at the party. The Vicar will be there and I will ask him to keep an eye on you. Any trouble and your father will hear about it when he comes home. He is not going to be at all pleased to hear about the fights you have been in since we moved here."

Hugh looks insulted. "The other boys always start it," he retorts.

"What nonsense! That is quite enough of that. Now just be quiet and get on with your tea."

She has told us many times that once the War ended there

135

will be World Peace and our father will return. The War has ended, she tells us that there is now World Peace, but there is still no sign of our father. She told me that he was missing when I was born; now he is missing when I am going to my first party.

"What can I wear?" I ask.

"Why don't you wear the pale-blue frilly party frock?"

"Oh, Nan, it's horrid! You know how scratchy it is. When I wore it last Christmas it made me cry, don't you remember?" I whine.

"Yes, I do; I do remember, and yes, it did chafe your neck badly. Let's see if I can remove the neck frill, that will be more comfy, won't it? If I unpick it, will you hem it, Mum?" She agrees and asks Nan to pin a note on the neck reminding her of the alteration to be made. I feel a bit happier about having to wear it; although with its layers and layers of frills I know that I will look a bit soppy in it.

"You look so sweet in pale blue with your colouring," Nan remarks. I know that she is trying to make me feel better about wearing this awful frock.

"Yes, you looks very sweet in pale blue ..." Hugh begins.

"Stop it, Hugh, stop it this minute," she says crossly, knowing that he is going to tease me. "If you have finished your tea, you can go and feed the dog and the cat whilst we get on with the frocks."

He leaves and we open the summer trunk and get on with the female business of party clothes.

"What about this one?" asks Felicity, pulling a black satin sheath covered in sequins out of the trunk?

"Whatever next, Felicity? That was one of the very special evening gowns that were part of my trousseau. It looked marvellous when I wore it to The Ritz on my honeymoon but it is not suitable for this event. Fold it up carefully, yes, use the tissue paper and then lay it on the table. Can you imagine anyone, let alone a young girl of fifteen, wearing that to the Working Men's Club?" she laughs artificially. Felicity looks sulky.

"Working Men's Club?" Nanny repeats, alarm ringing in her voice. "Is that where the party is being held? Do you think the children should to go? You know how much the men dr..."

136

"It will be alright, Nan dear, the Vicar will be there and the American Red Cross officials so don't worry. The party will be such a treat for them and, of course, the men won't be allowed to be at the Club whilst it is going on."

"This one is very pretty," Nan smiles at Felicity and pulls out a long, emerald green silk.

"Yes, that is a possibility," my mother agrees. She holds it up against my sister. "I can shorten the sleeves, take up the hem and take it in at the waist. What do you think, Nan?" she asks. "Turn around Felicity and let me see the back." She fiddles with the back and then spins my big sister around to face her.

"Now, before I put in all the work of re-making this gown, do you like it? Do you like the colour? Will you wear it when it is finished? Emerald green goes well with your black hair, and you can wear those silver shoes Aunt Molly gave us; they should still fit you." Felicity agrees that it will be suitable and thanks Mother for saying that she will alter it. She is then told to stand up on the chair so that the hem can be measured and she replies that she is far too old to stand on the chair like a Little One and Mother replies that she is far too old to kneel on the bricks to mark the hem. Up Felicity climbs and Mother calls out the alterations to be made and Nan writes them on a small piece of paper, which she then pins it the frock.

"Elizabeth can wear that pretty Viyella frock that you smocked, Nan."

"Oh, Mum, I don't think that she should go; she is far too

 young. I think that she should stay here with us and she and the baby can have their afternoon sleep." They agree, and so Lizzybuff, Ted and Charlotte are going to miss all the excitement.

Whilst they are very all busy with Felicity's gown, Lizzybuff and I are dressing up in some of the things from the trunk. I have on my mother's black hat and her long black gown and I am holding one of her evening bags. Lizzybuff drapes herself in the satin cloak with the blue lining and puts one of our old summer hats on her head. We are having a grand time, traipsing around behind my mother's back draped in her finery, when she turns around and sees us.

"Whatever are you doing, you two? Take those things off at once, this isn't a dressing-up game, it is serious business. Take those clothes off them Felicity, please, and fold them and put them back in the trunk. I think they had better go to bed early, they are getting over-excited." We quietly help her pack away the things in the trunk.

Nan says, "I'll take them up to bed now and read them a story to calm them down after all the excitement. Fancy, a real party after all these years! We have all had such a busy day, so why don't put your feet up in the drawing room Mum, and have a rest and I'll call you when supper is ready."

Chapter 27
The Red Cross Party

Felicity's gown is finished and she has cleaned our shoes ready for the party. Saturday finally arrives, by which time I feel quite sick with excitement. Nan makes me have a rest after lunch and then gets me ready for the party, which, she tells me, starts at 2 o'clock. "Now, Henny," she says, tucking a clean handkerchief under the leg elastic of my knickers, "behave yourself and remember the magic words, 'please' and 'thank you' and," she smiles at me, "don't ask too many questions! I have asked Felicity to look after you and I am sure that you will have an exciting time."

The three of us cross the road and walk down the lane to the Club. We shake hands with the lady at the door who is wearing a white uniform with a big red cross on her chest and go inside. Other Grown-Ups in uniform organize us into playing games. We play Pass the Parcel, Musical Chairs, What's the Time, Mr. Wolf? This game was quite scary and I trip over a chair trying to get away from Mr. Wolf, who was really David, the butcher's son, but I manage not to cry because if I do Felicity might take me home. Then they play some American games but, because I don't know how to play them, I stand by the wall and look around.

At the end of the hall I can see the food laid out on long tables covered with big white tablecloths. I move closer. I have never, ever seen so much food in my whole life. It looks as though all the food in the world is on those tables. There are big plates piled high with sandwiches with the crusts cut off. I have never seen a piece of bread with the crusts cut off. Why have they cut them off? Where are they? Could I ask to take them home for my rabbits? I feel quite funny at the idea that they might have been thrown away. Wasting food is what my mother calls a crime and it is a very bad thing to do.

There are plates of iced buns, a very big cake with little flags and candles, big white jugs of milk each with a red cross on the side, brown covered biscuits and then piles of what look like orange balls. I am nearly overcome by the sight of so much to eat.

If only my horrid party frock had pockets I could take some sandwiches home for the rabbits.

At that moment the bossy ladies tell us to line up and they will help each of us fill our plates. When it comes to my turn I let the officer put as much food as will fit on my plate. She leans down and tells me that they will light the candles on the cake after we have all finished eating and then we can have a slice of cake too. "Here you are," she says, handing me one of the orange-coloured balls.

"What is it, please?" I ask.

"Bless my soul!" the woman exclaims turning to the staff person next to her, "this child doesn't know what an orange is! Have you never seen one before?" she asks.

"No, never. What is it, please?"

"It is a fruit from America; you peel the skin off and you eat it. It's delicious; it's an orange, the fruit they make your National Orange Juice from." I point to a dish of brown covered biscuits. "And those are chocolate cookies, dear." I thank her and she adds one to my plate. I carry my feast to an empty seat at one of the tables. The hall is silent because there is just so much to eat nobody wastes any time talking. When we have finished and our plates are empty, the candles on the cake are lit and everyone claps and cheers. The cake is cut and the ladies bring us each a piece. It is very sweet and very delicious. Some of the children lick their plates clean but I know that I mustn't do that because if Vicar sees me he will tell my mother.

The tables are cleared and the crumbs brushed up and then we are each handed a white shoebox with a red cross printed on the lid. It is announced that every box has been filled with gifts collected by the Red Cross from people all over the United States of America. There are boxes for girls and boxes for boys and for different age groups too. It all sounds very important and it is exciting to get presents from people you don't even know, just like the time we had received a big parcel of dried fruit from strangers in Canada, which had been such a treat. That parcel was filled with raisins, currants and sultanas and some fruits called dried apricots, all things I had never tasted before. We just ate a few at a time and they seemed to last for ever.

I open my box and pull out a huge golden-coloured slithery satin scarf with printing on it and a man in a hat on a horse in one corner. I am sitting next to a skinny, badly dressed, freckle-faced girl named Ellie, who, I know is a 'vacuee' from the slums of London. I ask her what the word in the corner of the scarf says. "Can't you read?" she asks. "How old are you?"

"I am five," I reply, "but I am not allowed to learn to read yet because I am going to be a famous artist."

"Cor blimey!" she exclaims, shaking her scraggly ginger plaits, "my Aunty Joan's right, you are a toffee-nosed, stuck-up bunch! Famous artist, my foot!"

"What does it say?" I persist.

"Texas!"

I thank her politely, wondering what Texas is but don't like to ask. Next I take out a small wooden shoe with a painting of a windmill on the front, then a big colouring book with drawings already in it, a bag of glass marbles and finally a shell, which I like very much. It is big and shiny and has white spots on a black and brown background. One of the ladies tells me to that if I put it up to my ear I will be able to hear the sea so I do and I can hear a rushing sort of noise, which I suppose is the sea, but never having been to the seaside I don't really know.

A large lady officer claps her hands and announces that now tea is over we must all pack our gifts neatly back in their boxes.

The Vicar gives a vote of thanks to the Red Cross and then we all stand to attention whilst the Grown-Ups sing the National Anthem of the United States of America and then *God Save the King*. When it is finished most of the children rush home to tell their families all about this amazing party.

Felicity, Hugh and I politely thank the officer at the door, say goodbye to the Vicar and leave clutching our boxes and the bag of oranges.

It is exciting showing our mother and Nan the gifts we have received. Hugh has a pair of socks, which he was not pleased with, but my mother is; a hard rubber ball, a book about aeroplanes, a shiny new penknife and a pack of cards. Felicity has a packet of embroidered handkerchiefs, a long green scarf, a shiny brooch, a book about ballet and a long length of blue silk ribbon. I show them my gifts and they admire the shell and Nan says she likes my scarf and says that the man on the horse is called a cowboy.

"We had chocolate biscuits!" Hugh exclaims, "I remember chocolate, we had it before the War, didn't we, Mother? I'd forgotten what it tasted like. We had cake and biscuits and jam and lots and lots of yummy food, and we brought these home." He dramatically empties our oranges out onto the table.

"Real oranges!" Nan exclaims. 'Well, I never did! You really are very lucky children."

Suddenly, I feel a bit funny. "Nan, quick! I'm going to be sick!" Nanny grabs me and rushes me off to the cloakroom at the end of the hallway. We arrive just in time.

"I think that you ate too much, Henny, and maybe you were a bit over-excited. There you are, let me wash your face and hands. Are you feeling better now? Yes? That's good, now you had better sit down very quietly and play with your new presents and you will soon feel much better." She leads me back into the kitchen.

"Is she all right, Nan?" Mother enquires. Nan replies that she thinks I will be alright now.

"That was such a nice party," I tell her, hugging my box to my chest, sighing with contentment, "and the best food in all the world." Then I remember, "Nan, they had cut off all the crusts from the sandwiches..."

"Don't you worry about that, Henny; Americans have different ways of doing things. Just think instead about the party and all the lovely things you ate," she smiles lovingly at me, "even," she adds more to herself, "if they did make you sick!"

Chapter 28
The Holiday

My mother is weeping. She is holding a letter in her hand and tears are streaming down her face. I pretend not to see her as Ted and I creep past the open drawing room door.

Grown-Ups never cry, whatever is wrong? How very worrying, should I tell Nan? Perhaps she can happy her up.

We slip out of the back door and head for the barn. I call Briggs but he is nowhere to be seen so I give Betty a quick beating, chew a few of the black things, nibble the eraser and begin to feel better.

My mother stayed in her room for the next few days and we seldom saw her. Nan told us that we had to be especially good and quiet because her nerves were bad and she was feeling sad and depressed.

Some days later she appeared at breakfast and said she had some news. "I had a letter from your father and he says that he cannot return home until October, even though the War is over. Now that we know that he will not be home yet I have decided that, after nearly five and a half years of Wartime, we all deserve a good holiday. I have rented a house in a small village in Wales for a month.

"What's a holiday?" I ask. "What is Wales?"

Before she can reply, Hugh informs me that Wales is a country stuck onto the side of England. "Don't you know what a holiday is?" he sneers.

"How could she know, Hugo? We have not been on a holiday since before she was born. You may well remember going to Cornwall when you were small, but that was long before the War.

"We have lots of preparation to do!" Nan exclaims. "Perhaps you can make some of your famous lists, Mum?"

She agrees and then says that we will be returning home two days before Hugo and Felicity go back to school for the winter term, so before we leave they have to get all their school books and clothes and other bits and pieces ready.

"Felicity, please can you iron Hugh's school shirts as well

143

as your own? It will be such a help as Nan and I are so busy. If any of them need mending, his, I mean, not yours, because I know you look after your clothes properly," she smiles at my big sister and scowls at Hugh, "put them to one side and Nan and I will mend them before we leave for Wales. Now what about your school shoes, dearest? If they need mending you had better take them to the cobbler before we go. Hugh, bring me yours and I will see if they are worth getting repaired in which case you can go with Felicity and see if Mr. White thinks he can fix them. I know your feet are growing fast and you really need a new pair but Felicity must have a new mackintosh, which will use up eleven coupons, so I don't know if we will have enough left to buy shoes for you. Hopefully, Aunt Molly will send us some more of your cousins' hand-me-downs soon. There will be no time at all to get anything done when we return, so everything for school must be finished before next Friday."

Hugh looks very unhappy at the thought of the summer holidays ending but cheers up a bit when she tells us that we will travel to Wales by train.

"I'll take my books of train numbers. There will be lots of engine numbers to collect at Patisford Station. Which line is it to Wales?"

"I don't know, Hugo. Great Western Railway I expect. Why don't you bicycle over to Wentley Station this morning? I'll write down the name of the Welsh village where we will be staying, it has a very long name beginning with two L's. You can ask the Station Master which line we will travel on, he should know, or if he doesn't he can look it up for you. Ask him to write down for me the trains we have to catch and their times."

Hugh finishes his fried bread as fast as he can and rushes off to get his books and his bike. He says that he is a bit worried because his front tyre is going bald and so Mother advises him to ride slowly and avoid stones and any rough patches in the road.

Felicity leaves the table saying that she is very pleased about the holiday and that she is going upstairs to decide which clothes and books to take and will also start getting her school things ready. Later she will iron the shirts and help with anything else that needs doing before we leave.

"Thank you, Felicity; I am sure there will be all sorts of things we will need help with. Now, Nan, as long as Henrietta does not start asking endless questions, we can have some peace and quiet! I really do wonder sometimes, whether this child will ever run out of her seemingly unending supply of questions!"

"Why don't you draw all your favourite buttons from the bowl at Miss Emily's shop once you have finished your breakfast? Here's a piece of paper. Before we leave I want you to bring me your little crochet bag and we will pack your pencils and I'll make you a small drawing book and then you can draw me pictures whilst we are on holiday. I couldn't find the eraser when I looked in my desk for it, I don't know where it is and we really do need it in case you make mistakes."

I hope she never finds out that I took it to eat.

I start my drawing and listen as they chat happily whilst Nan gives Charlotte her bottle and Mother cuts up Lizzybuff's toast into strips and feeds it to her, soldier by soldier.

"Can I take my dungarees, please?" They both agree that that is a good idea. "Can Ted come? Please?" I add. She says that, because Ted has been so well behaved lately, he should be allowed to come with us on the holiday. I thank her, and pressing my luck, ask if Clementina and just one tiny rabbit can come as well.

"Don't be silly, Henrietta," Mother replies, "and before you ask, Briggs will take care of everything whilst we are away, all the animals and the house and the garden, and," she adds, "the allotments too. Now, sit up at the table and get on with your drawing. Draw some more buttons and then colour them for me. Nan and I have to get on with planning the holiday. We only have a few days to get everything organized. I must not forget the Identity Cards, Nan, and of course the Ration Books too. I wonder how much longer everything will be rationed?"

At last it is Friday. Our bags are all packed and we are ready to catch the before-breakfast bus to Patisford. When it arrives, Briggs helps Hugh load the luggage. Felicity and Hugh go upstairs but, because we have Lizzybuff and Charlotte with us, the Grown-Ups, Ted and I sit downstairs. Ted is wearing his best jersey and his blue trousers and I am wearing my favourite sky-blue frock, which has had the hem let down because I am growing so fast. Nan is in her grey afternoon uniform even though it is still morning and my mother, a dark brown frock with an odd pink thing at her neck that she calls a jabot.

"Hold tight, Ted, we're going over the bump," I cry and the bus flies over it very fast, much to our delight.

We soon arrive at the bus station and the Big Ones unload our suitcases with help from the conductor and we all wait together whilst our mother strides down the platform to hail a taxi. The luggage is placed in the boot and we pile in for the short journey to the railway station.

A porter loads the luggage onto his cart whilst she buys our tickets. "Platform 3," says the Ticket Inspector as he clips a hole in each of them. "Change at Bristol for Temple Mead," he adds. She thanks him and we follow the porter onto the platform.

Suddenly, there is a tremendous thundering, chuffing noise and a huge black engine comes along the track towards us. Ted and I hide behind Nan and cling to her skirt. The awful noise and the smoke swirling all around us is very scary, like being in a really bad dream. Nan squeezes my shoulder and holds onto me until the train comes to a shuddering stop. The porter helps us up into the carriage and then stows some of the luggage in the racks above our heads and puts the rest in the guard's van. The doors are slammed, the guard blows his whistle, waves his red flag and the train chuffs out of the station.

I watch out of the window as the train gathers speed and we soon leave Patisford behind. The countryside rushes by and the procession of tiny farms and flocks of sheep and rivers and villages enchant me.

"Look," shouts Hugh suddenly, pointing out of the window. "Look, Mother, gypsies!" She stands up and goes over to the window and I rush over to see them.

"Oh! Just look at those horse-drawn caravans. Six of them; that really is a very large family and look at all their dogs, lurchers they are called, and only gypsies have that type of dog. I wonder where they are going. No, they are not our gypsies, Henrietta; they are far too far off the Plain."

"We never did go and see them at the camp did we, Mum? I wonder how that child's arm is."

"We have been so busy, Nan, haven't we? Maybe when we return they will be back in the village again and then we will see if we can find time one afternoon to walk up to their encampment."

I continue to watch the passing scenery for ages with my nose pressed against the dirty window and then, worn out with all the excitement, I climb up onto the seat and fall fast asleep.

Nan wakes me and tells me that we have to change trains, which we do and then as soon as we are settled in the new train I fall to sleep again.

When I finally wake up Hugh tells me that we have been under the sea. I have no idea what he is talking about and ask Nan if he's telling fibs. "No, Henny," she replied, "we did go under the sea in a long, long tunnel."

"Why?"

"It is the only way to get to Wales by train," Mother explains. "We will soon be in Cardiff and then we only have to take one more train and we will be there."

I am too sleepy to ask more questions and so I sit and think about it for a while. I look across at Hugh, who is looking out of the window, looking unhappy. Felicity is reading and both the Little Ones are still asleep. I stand up and look out of his window and I cannot believe my eyes. Instead of more fields and cows and farmyards there are broken houses, real houses all smashed to pieces with broken windows. Some have their chimneys leaning over; whole sides of some houses are missing. There are piles of rubble everywhere; beds half hanging out of damaged bedrooms, curtains askew, torn wallpaper, a toy cupboard just like ours burst open with all the toys and books strewn among the rubble. We pass a street were one whole house is unhurt and every other one is shattered, completely destroyed. Next, a church with the steeple lying on the ground and I can see all the pews smashed up and lying all over the church floor amidst piles of hymn books. There are signs of bad fires in some streets; we pass a school with no roof, a burned out car, trees blasted to pieces, and garden sheds reduced to piles of tin and planks, the tools and lawnmowers scattered all over the wrecked gardens.

"Whatever happened, Nan?" I gasp, tears pouring down my cheeks. "Why is everything smashed up? What happened to the childr…"

Mother interrupts before Nanny can answer. "The City of Cardiff was very heavily bombed in the War, Henrietta," she informs me.

Nan hugs Ted and me tightly to her. "It's alright, Henny, the War is over now and it won't ever happen again. There will be no more bombing, it's all over."

"Now," says Mother before I can ask any more questions, "It is time to get ready as we will soon arrive at the station. Hugo take down the picnic basket and the other items from the rack and when we get to the station find a porter and make sure he takes all our bags out of the guard's van. We will meet you, and the luggage, at the restaurant. Ask the porter to wheel it inside and then I will give him a tip."

We enter the restaurant and a thin, tired-looking, young waitress comes to take our order. At the same time the porter enters with Hugo and the suitcases. "You can't bring that in here," she yells at him above the din, "leave that luggage outside."

Mother tells Hugh to wait outside with the porter and the bags. "I will send you out a glass of milk," she adds.

"No milk," snaps the waitress. I pull my chair in closer to the table and the legs scrape on the linoleum making a loud squeaking noise. "Stop it," she screams, "stop it, don't move that chair, stop that noise. I just can't take it any more!" and she bursts into tears and collapses on the floor.

I am horrified and am about to jump down to help her get up when Mother says very sternly "Sit back on your seat and don't take any notice, Henrietta." Out of the corner of my eye I see another waitress pull the poor woman up and take her away.

"Whatever did I do, Nan?" I ask, both puzzled and alarmed.

"It's all right Henny, it's not your fault. She must be shell-shocked from all the bombing and her nerves are bad."

"I didn't mean to make her cry."

"Hush, darling, just sit still and it will soon be time to catch the next train. I do hope that she," Nan glances at me and then looks across and addresses Mother, "won't have nightmares about all this . . . "

Nightmares? This was all much worse than any I had ever had. Maybe this was where Ellen and her children lived? Maybe it was here that they were bombed and killed and maybe their house fell down too and all their toys fell out into the garden and got spoilt?

"She'll be all right, Nan. Once we have left all this destruction behind and are settled in the village out in the countryside she will soon forget about it."

Hugh comes into the restaurant and tells us that our train is waiting on Platform 6 and that the bags are already stowed in the guard's van and that he has already managed to collect quite a few new engine numbers.

We climb up into a much smaller train and it soon leaves the station. There are more bombed-out houses on both sides of the carriage and I start to cry, heartbroken as we pass yet another church that has become a pile of rubble; there are fragments of stained glass still in the broken windows catching the sunlight. Then we pass a factory with no roof, a school with no windows, and yet more toys lying in the rubbish outside a row of gutted houses.

"Let me have Charlotte, Nan. Elizabeth you go and sit by Felicity. Felicity, please stop reading for just a few minutes and see to the Little One, and Nan, put Henrietta on your knee and see if you can comfort her. Climb up onto Nanny's lap, child, and stop fretting. We are all meant to be happy; we are going on holiday," she says, rather crossly. Hugh continues to stare silently out of the window. Ted and I snuggle up against Nanny's soft bosom and we soon fall asleep again safe within her arms, completely worn out with all the horror of the bomb damage.

Chapter 29
Wales

"Wake up, Henny! We are nearly there," Nan says cheerfully. "Look at the green fields and trees; we are safely back in the countryside." The train pulls into a tiny station and a porter opens the door and helps us out. The Guard unloads our suitcases and the Station Master comes along the platform to meet us.

"Good afternoon, ma'am," he raises his cap to my mother, "you must be the family who have come to stay in the Doctor's house. Welcome to our village. Evans the taxi is waiting for you and Mrs. Gwynne, the Doctor's housekeeper will be at the house to greet you." He smiles at Hugh.

"And you, young man, I expect you collect train numbers don't you? You are welcome to come to my station any time you like, four trains a day on the down line and three on the up. Maybe you can help me with the ticketing and some of the other jobs? I could use your help, it's been difficult with everyone away at the War, and even though it is now over many of the lads have not returned yet." Hugh looks as though he will burst with excitement. He looks up at my mother and, seeing her nod in agreement, promises to return the next morning.

The taxi stops and we scramble out in front of a very tall thin white house with steps leading up to a black front door, which swings open and there is an old woman smiling at us. "Welcome, ma'am," she says, "and welcome to you, Nanny, and to all the family. Welcome to the Doctor's house. I am Mrs. Gwynne, the housekeeper, and I will look after you all whilst you are here. I will do all the cooking and the housework and so you, Nanny, will only have the children to look after." Nan looks very surprised and blushes with pleasure. "Bring in the luggage, Evans," she orders.

"Come this way, please." She leads us into a large drawing room, which has a wide bay window looking down on the street and then into the dining room. She says that when she has shown us all over the house she will serve tea in the dining room. She points out the cloakroom and then the Doctor's Office, which is kept locked in his absence. She tells us her rooms are next to the kitchen and that she has lived in this house serving the doctor and his wife for the last thirty years.

"It will be enjoyable for me to have some young children around again," she says smiling at us." All our children are grown up and gone away, married they are, with children of their own. There are still some of their toys upstairs for you all to play with, and," she adds, looking at Felicity, "there are lots of Deirdre's books in your bedroom. I expect you read a lot, don'y you?" She agrees and looks excited. "There are all sorts of games in the cupboard in Jonathan's old room like Monopoly, Ludo, Drafts, Snakes and Ladders and a few more. And," she looks at Hugh, "you'll find something very special in his old bedroom, just you wait and see."

"Now let's go upstairs." There is a big bedroom in the front of the house for Mother, then one that is locked, and she says the next one will be our night nursery. There is a smaller one for each of the Big Ones. There are lots of books waiting for Felicity to read in her room and in Hugh's, to his delight, there is a very large wooden fort with boxes of toy soldiers on the shelf beside it. In our new night nursery there is a rocking horse, whose name, Mrs. Gwynne tells me, is Tony. She says that I can ride him if Nan helps me up onto his back.

Hugh rushes up the stairs that lead from the bedroom floor to the garden and then rushes back down again. "Wow!" he exclaims, "you should see the garden. It's smashing! There's a bamboo forest, a super big lawn, lots of trees to climb and a vegetable garden with a high wall around it. You have to go up these stairs to the very top of the house and then over a very narrow bridge to get into the garden." He is shaking with excitement and having imparted this information he tears off back upstairs again.

"Well, that does sound exciting, doesn't it?" says Mother. "Maybe we can have tea when it is ready, Mrs. Gwynne? It seems a long time since we had sandwiches in Cardiff Station and afterwards we will all go up to see the garden."

The housekeeper suggests that we first go and see her kitchen which is in the basement. It is very large and rather damp. To my joy there is a big fat, fluffy ginger cat sitting in front of the range.

"That there is Marmalade," she tells us. "He's a good mouser but a bit lazy, if you ask me, but he's good company on a cold winter's night." Marmalade blinks sleepily at me and I hope that he and I will soon become good friends.

She opens the back door and shows us the washing yard and is just closing the door when we hear Hugh calling us. "Wherever is he, Nan?"

"Up here!" Hugh yells. "Up here in the garden!" We look up and there, way up in the sky, is Hugh, looking over the edge of the garden wall. "This is where the garden is, and that," he points, "is the tiny bridge you have to cross."

"Well I never!" Nanny exclaims. "Fancy having the garden above the roof! I've never heard of such a thing in all my born days. This is a funny upside down house, I must say."

"That is because it is built into the side of a cliff," replies my mother knowledgeably. "Come on down, Hugo, and have your tea." Huffing and puffing with excitement, he reappears but is so thrilled with all that he has seen so far that he does not eat nearly as much as usual.

After tea he leads us up the stairs to a narrow landing at the end of which there is a small door. It is dark and cobwebby and a bit frightening. Hanging on the back of the door is an old brown garment. "Good heavens!" exclaims Mother, "it is an old monk's habit, how very odd. Earlier I found a loaded pistol in the drawer of my dressing table. What a strange house this is."

"Where is the pistol? Can I see it?" asks Hugh.

"No, you cannot; I gave it to Mrs. Gwynne and she locked it in the Doctor's office."

He pushes open the little door. "That's the bridge you have to cross," he shouts, "it's very narrow, and very scary. You'll have to carry Lizzybuff, Nan, or she will fall. Here let me hold your arm. Don't look down, Henny, or you will fall right down into the washing yard, splat, and will be strawberry jam!"

I look down and there is a sheer drop to the washing yard. "Nan," I whisper, "I can't go over it, I don't want to fall and be strawberry jam." I feel quite hysterical with fear.

"It's alright, Henny. Hugh, stop teasing her and carry the Little One across and take her into the garden and hold onto her tight. Maybe you had better go next, Felicity and make sure Hugh doesn't leave Lizzybuff on her own in the garden. Mum, can you carry the baby for me? Thank you. Now, Henny, stand in front of me and I will hold you and Ted very tightly and you just walk across. Don't look down. Look at Hugh's face and we'll soon be across." She looks up, "No, Hugh, this is not the time to make faces at her, she really is scared, after all she's only five."

Finally, we are all safely across the bridge and walk up the steep steps into the garden. Hugh tears off and returns at great speed yelling: "It's magic, it's a magic garden," he shouts, twirling around and around with his arms stretched out as though he's an aeroplane. "Look at the bamboo forest; you can make a house in there Henny. There's a summer house and there are two old bath chairs in there and we can use them for races. Felicity you can push Lizzybuff and I'll push Henny and we can race around and around the whole garden. This is the best holiday ever!" Felicity looks rather bored at the idea but Hugh's enthusiasm is catching and we are all soon thrilled with this very special garden. We walk across the lawn to the far end where there is a low wall and when we look over it we can see the whole village below and there is a black cow standing in a large pond. "That's a bull," Hugh shouts, "I bet he's very fierce."

"How do you know it's a bull and not a cow, Hugh?" Felicity asks, scornfully.

"Because," he pauses, "if you see one cow by itself, it's always a bull," he replies, nodding his head to emphasize such an indisputable fact.

"Look, Mum, that must be at least a fifty foot drop down this cliff to the village. The Little Ones mustn't come over here at all, do you hear that Henny, you are NOT to come over here by yourself," Nan says, firmly.

"Hugo, do not lean over like that and you must never try to climb down the other side, do you hear me?" He nods his head. "If you fell down that cliff you would be killed. Nan, the agent for the house said that there is a playpen so we will have to keep

153

the Little Ones in that when we are out here."

"I'm not a Little One," I protest loudly, "please don't put me in the playpen. I promise I won't go near the wall."

"Now it is time to return to the house and get settled in," Mother says, changing the subject. "Hugo, go and see if you can find another way into the house without going over that awful bridge." He rushes off at top speed, arms outstretched, and making loud revving noises. Lizzybuff and I pick daisies while we wait.

Eventually he returns and comes to a screeching halt at my mother's feet. "No! There is no other way in, unless we put a rope ladder over this wall..."

"That is quite enough stupidness, Hugo. I am sure that we will soon become accustomed to using the bridge. Do you think that you could rig up some rope across for us to hold onto?" He agrees that he can probably fix something up. We cross very carefully with Nan holding Ted and me tightly to her once more. The house seems very dark and gloomy after the brightness of the enchanted sunlit garden.

Chapter 30
The Garden in the Sky

We soon settle into a routine and spend most of our days in the garden. Sometimes I draw whilst Mother embroiders and Nan knits. Lizzybuff and Charlotte play happily in the playpen.

"This really is idyllic after all the problems of the War years, isn't it, Nan? It's so peaceful and it is such a wonderful change and the children are enjoying themselves so much. I am thankful that I decided that we should have a holiday, we certainly deserved it!" she laughs and Nan agrees with her.

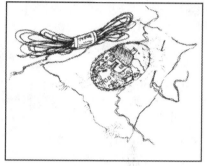

Nan has let Lizzybuff out of the playpen and she is busy collecting daisies for me to make her a daisy chain. I am allowed to explore the garden as long as I keep away from the wall. Felicity sits in a deckchair and reads endlessly, although she does join in the bath chair races around and around the lawn once or twice. I have to hang on very tight because Hugh is such a reckless driver but, of course, we win every race. The weather is sunny and warm enough for us to wear our swimming costumes and we never do get to play any board games because we spend all our time playing in the garden.

At breakfast one morning Mrs. Gwynne tells us that it has just been announced on the wireless that today is the end of the War in Japan, VJ Day. Mother and Nan look very pleased but this time I don't ask her about our father returning because she was so cross when I asked her before.

Ted and I are sitting on the picnic rug beside my mother's deck chair. I ask her if she will tell me her story about the polo ponies.

"Your father had several polo ponies," she begins, "and we rose at 5 o'clock every day and went riding in the desert in the cool of the morning."

"How many ponies did you have?"

"I can't remember," Mother replied. "Now, I will continue if you are going to listen and stop asking questions." I smile at her sweetly and nod my head. "We went to many parties at the Officer's Mess in the evenings and I had my new friends to tea and we had bridge parties and I played tennis. I drew and painted and worked on my embroidery in the evenings whilst your father read to me. What happy times those were."

"Tell me about going on twek," I demand.

"Trek, child, not twek, T-R-E-K," seeing my blank look she said she had forgotten I did not know how to spell.

"Sit still and I will tell you. One day your father announced that he had to go to one of the outlying districts to see about some problem or another and I was very excited about this adventure. I knew by then that I was going to have a baby so I had to be extra careful not to get too tired. We left long before dawn one morning, your father and I on horseback and the servants and some of his soldiers followed in bullock carts filled with all our food and equipment for a week's trek. The Southern Cross was huge in the sky and, because there were no lights anywhere at night, the stars were amazingly bright, millions and millions of them. When the moon was full we could see for miles.

"We travelled towards the mountains and finally reached a plateau with mountains on three sides and we camped there because it was cool and shady. The next morning, as we were setting off, I saw this little tree with pink flowers and told your father that I wanted it for our garden. One of the servants started to dig it up and then your father, who was scanning the mountains with his binoculars, told the man to stop digging and that we had to leave at once. One of his soldiers had informed him that the local tribesmen, who were watching us from the mountainsides, considered the nuba tree sacred and therefore, had we dug it up, they would have been very angry. We quickly moved out of the valley leaving the tree behind and continued on our trek.

"The last day we camped in a deserted oasis. We were not aware that our water rations had run out and, without your father's knowledge, the servants had drawn water from the well, and had served it to us. I soon became very sick and then he discovered the reason. There was a dead donkey in the bottom of the well. He rushed me back to the camp and put me into the Military Hospital.

"Once I recovered, I was sent back to England, leaving my beloved husband and my exotic new life behind.

"It was a long, sad journey and the end of my great adventure. My dear father met me at the docks and soon I was home again and in his care. Your big sister, Felicity, was born some months later. She was more than a year old by the time your father returned to England on leave."

On Sunday morning Hugh goes down to the station to help with some crates that have to be put on the up train. Nan agrees that I can take Lizzybuff and Ted for a walk around the garden to look for butterflies. We wander around for a while and then come to the door of the walled garden. The door is propped open with a stick. "Lizzybuff, hold my hand and I'll help you up the steps."

Inside there are rows and rows of vegetables and rows of sweet peas, which an elderly woman is picking. When she sees us she runs off, cackling to herself. Sweet peas are Mother's favourite flowers, especially the bright red and the pale mauve ones mixed together, so I pick a bunch for her.

We follow the brick path back to the door, only to find that it is closed. I can't reach the handle and so there is no way that I can open it. I look around for the woman but there is no sign of her. Lizzybuff begins to cry. "I want my Nanny," she snivels

"She's not your Nanny, she's mine," I retort unkindly, which only makes her cry more.

"Open the door," she whimpers.

"I can't. It's stuck. We'll have to climb up over the wall. I'll push you up onto the barrel that's leaning against the wall and then I'll climb up after you." I tuck Ted into the top of my waistband and somehow we both manage to get up onto the barrel. Once there I push Lizzybuff up onto the flat top of the wall and I pull myself up too and sit beside her. I look down and, to my horror, see that the ground is way, way below us.

"It's too far to jump, Lizzybuff, we'll have to call Nan to

come and get us." Unfortunately, at that moment Ted somehow wriggles free and tumbles down to the ground. "Oh! No! He must have broken his leg," I cry in distress. "Now hold onto me tight, Lizzybuff, or you will fall down just like poor Ted did and break your leg too." She begins to snivel and then to cry as we sit holding on to each other precariously balanced on the wall. We call Nan and when she doesn't come we shout. Eventually, when there is still no sight of her, we scream, louder and louder. Then we begin to shriek.

Meanwhile, the Grown-Ups are relaxing in deck chairs in the shade of the bamboo forest whilst Charlotte plays happily in the playpen. Hugh, of course, is still down at the station and Felicity has gone fishing in the pond below the wall.

"I wonder whose children are screaming like that. What bad manners, making such a noise on a Sunday!"

Nanny suddenly sits bolt upright. "By the way, where

are Henrietta and Elizabeth? They have been gone a long time. Oh, Mum, you don't think that it is our children screaming, do you?" She scrambles to her feet and rushes off in the direction of the alarming noise. When she sees us perched on top of the wall she looks very worried. "Just keep absolutely still, darlings, don't move an inch and I'll soon get you down."

"Ted has fallen and broken his leg, Nan," I sob.

"Don't be silly, Henny, he's fine. You know that knitted teddy bears can't break their legs! Now try and calm Lizzybuff down and hold onto her very tight." She walks up the steps and opens the door by the handle.

"There was a stick in it Nan, and then somehow it fell out and the wind slammed it shut and we couldn't get out."

She places a big stone against the door and then climbs up onto the barrel and lifts us down onto it one by one. Once we are all back on the ground she blows our noses, wipes our tears, gives us both a big hug and then gently leads us out of the walled garden and down the steps. Lizzybuff is still sobbing.

"That must have given you both a terrible fright," she says, "but you are alright now that your dear Nanny has rescued you." I pick up Ted, who is lying flat on his back in the grass, brush him off and hug him and we walk back to my mother, holding Nan's hands.

"What a dreadful noise, Henrietta, whatever was wrong? Making such a noise on a Sunday! Great heavens above, whatever will the village think?"

"They were very frightened, Mum," Nan explains quietly, "they were perched on top of that high wall and we are very lucky that they did not fall off."

"Whatever were they doing up there in the first place?"

"The door slammed shut and we couldn't get out," I explain. "I picked you some sweet peas Mother, red ones and mauve ones, the colours you like best, but I left them on top of the wall. Nan, please can you climb back up and get them for me?"

"Come on everyone," Mother says, "it is time to go in. We will pick some more flowers another day. Come and help me put away the deckchairs in the summer house, Henrietta."

At breakfast Mother one morning announces that, because it is full moon, we will celebrate the end of the War by having our supper in the summer house up in the garden. "Mrs. Gwynne will keep an eye on the Little Ones whilst they sleep. You can all change into your night clothes and put your sandals on and then, after supper, you can play on the lawn."

Felicity, Hugh and I play hide and seek and all sorts of games chasing each other in and out of the moonlight and this evening is the best part of the holiday which, sadly, soon afterwards came to an end.

We travelled back under the sea in the tunnel and through the horrors of Cardiff and on through the gentle English landscape to Patisford.

Back home once more, Briggs meets us with the happy news that there is a whole new family of baby rabbits for me to name.

Chapter 31
Our Father's Return

It is autumn and the leaves on the trees have changed to all sorts of different colours. The Virginia creeper's leaves are now deep red and those on the winter heaven are orange and beginning to turn to red. It is getting colder every day.

"Today is going to be the happiest day of our lives!" Mother announces at breakfast one foggy October morning. Her eyes glitter with excitement. "Last night," she continues, "after you were all in bed, Mr. Collins came over from the shop with a telephone message for me," she pauses and beams at us all, "it was from your father."

"He called to say that he would be at Patisford Bus Station at three o'clock this afternoon. Yes, he is coming home at last!" She sighs happily. "My Beloved is finally returning."

"I want you Big Ones to go on the after-lunch bus to meet him and you will take Henrietta with you. You must wear your school uniforms, yes, I know it is Saturday, but you have to look your very best to meet your father after all this time and he will be wearing his uniform too," she adds as she sees that Hugh is about to object. "Nan, will you dress Henrietta in her best clothes? Yes, and the new mitts you knitted her and she can wear that beret that Aunt Molly gave us; it should match her blue coat."

"Now please hurry up and finish your breakfasts and then I want you all to help Nanny and me tidy up the house and make it look its very best to welcome your father home to. It is fortunate, Nan, that I asked Briggs to air all the clothes in the Colonel's wardrobe just last week, when it was so sunny and warm. When he comes in he can polish all the Colonel's boots and shoes and make sure his dressing room is in tiptop order. Just look at that fog! Briggs should be here by now, but with this bad weather he may well be late. What a nuisance on such a busy day!"

"That reminds me; please can you clean your shoes, Hugo's and Henrietta's for me, Felicity? You can't possibly meet your father with dirty shoes, he would be horrified."

"I will go and pick some leaves or any late flowers that I can find in the garden to put in the vases; Hugo you go and tidy up the tool shed. Henrietta, you tidy up the nursery and put all the books back on the shelves and the toys in the cupboard and then make sure that Elizabeth puts all her blocks back in their box. Nan, maybe it would be a good idea to put Charlotte in the play pen so she can nap whilst all this is going on."

"Oh, I am so excited! We will have such a happy time now the War is over and your father is back. We will be a real family once more, won't we Nan?" She rushes out of the room and we clear the table and do the washing up in the scullery.

"I am a bit frightened," I tell Nan, tugging at her skirt.

"Why, Henny? Of course you aren't frightened! You'll love having your father home again. He will be so pleased how well you have helped Briggs and I expect he will get even more

rabbits once he is settled in. Now let's go into the nursery and you tidy up whilst I iron your best frock and a pair of clean sheets for your mother's bed."

"Can I take Ted on the bus with me?" I ask her.

"No, darling, I don't think that is a good idea but why not dress him up too? Not in Betty's frock, but in the trousers I made him and his Christmas jersey and then you can show him to your father later on. Hurry up now and get on with your work and then you can see to Ted whilst you are having your rest."

What will our father be like, I wonder, yet again. My mother always tells us that he is the most wonderful, the very bravest and the most handsome man in the whole world, but in the photos I have seen of him I think that he looks rather fierce, even though she says he loves animals as much as I do. If we have more rabbits, will he let me choose all their names like Briggs does? Maybe I had better think up some more names on the way to Patisford.

I have my rest and then Nan helps me put on my best frock. Downstairs she puts on my outdoor clothes and then it is time to go and wait for the bus. I am worried about riding on the bus with the Big Ones. Sensing my anxiety, Nan tells them both to look after me properly and to make sure that I don't fall down the bus steps or get left behind. I squeeze her hand and she bends down and whispers that everything will be all right. The bus arrives and we are off but I don't enjoy the journey as much as I usually do when I go to town with my mother. I ask Felicity for some rabbit names but she was not willing to tell me any and goes back to reading her book. I still feel very anxious about meeting our father for the very first time.

Finally the bus arrives at the station and we clamber downstairs. There, a long way off at the very far end of the very long platform stands a huge man in army uniform with a red band around his hat. He is surrounded by a heap of army-coloured luggage.

"Oh! Please God, don't let that be our father," I pray silently and urgently.

Felicity and Hugh rush off down the platform leaving me behind. I watch as the man pats Felicity on the shoulder and shakes Hugh's hand. It is our father. God must have been too busy to hear my prayer. I walk slowly towards him, panicking inside.

"Hello, Henrietta!" he bellows and then, to my horror, he bends down, takes both my hands in one of his huge ones, and kisses my cheek. His moustache is prickly and makes me want to sneeze. I try to pull away but I cannot move. He finally lets go of my hands and I promptly plop down on my bottom.

"Get up!" hisses Felicity. "Whatever would Nanny say, sitting on the dirty platform?"

I scramble to my feet and grab her hand and hold on to it tightly. Our father asks Hugh to help the conductor load the baggage into the compartment of the waiting bus. We troop upstairs and our father and Hugh sit in the front seat and Felicity and I sit on the seat behind them.

"Well," he booms, "and how have you been behaving, Hugo? I hope that I will not hear from your mother that you have been fighting with the boys in the village, I trust?"

Hugh's ears turn pink as he fibs hard and assures this frightening Grown-Up that he has behaved very well since we moved to the new village. Then our father turns around and asks Felicity how she is doing at school and she tells him how well she has done in her exams and he seems pleased. He then turns to me and asks if I am a help to my mother and to Nanny. I smile nervously and mumble that I collect all the food for the rabbits and that I help Briggs a lot and that he is my best friend.

He gives a funny sort of noise and mutters that he will "see about that", and turns back to face the front of the bus. I sit back in my seat knowing that I have said something wrong but don't know what. I change the subject in my head and wonder if I can slip away after tea to have a private chat with 'Gustus. Then I go back to making my list of new rabbit names. Janet, Joy, Emerald, after the Gypsy girl, that would be a good name; Jimmy for a boy, Caroline, Mary, Joan... Cathy, yes that's a good one...

The bus draws up outside our house. Across the road my mother, Elizabeth and Nanny, with Charlotte in her arms, wait at the gate. Our father steps off the bus leaving Hugh and the conductor to handle the baggage. He crosses the road and takes my mother in his arms, kisses her passionately and actually lifts her feet off the ground. She is laughing and crying at the same time and they both seem very happy to see each other again.

I remember the story she had told me of another time, many years before, when he had returned from the desert and she was going to meet him at Waterloo Station the next afternoon. She dreamed she was running down the platform to meet him and threw herself into his arms. What had really happened was that, still asleep, she stood up on her bed, ran down the length of it, crashed off the end and hit the wardrobe, bruising her face very badly. When she did meet him the next day he couldn't even kiss her because her face hurt so much.

Our father then greets Nanny, shaking her hand and thanking her for looking after his family so well in his absence. He smiles down at Elizabeth who promptly hides behind Nan. He puts out his huge hand to touch Charlotte's tiny one and she bursts into tears and hides her face. "She's a bit shy, Colonel" Nan explains, "but she will soon get used to you, I'm sure."

Suddenly Poor Old Bunker rushes up barking furiously and

jumps up at our father and wags his tail like mad. Our father rubs his head and says how pleased he is to see him again. Poor Old Bunker gazes up at him with adoration in his eyes. We are all amazed at the dog's sudden burst of energy and it would seem that the reason that he has been so miserable is because he really did miss his master.

Meanwhile, Briggs appears. When our father notices him, Briggs jumps to attention and salutes. "At ease, Briggs," he barks. I notice that Briggs has his best uniform on instead of the old overalls he usually wears. "See to the luggage," he orders. Briggs salutes and picks up all the baggage and takes it through the washing yard into the house.

I ask Nan if I can go and help Briggs unpack, but before she can reply, our father roars, "No, you cannot. We need to talk, Sylvia, about this child. It sounds as though she has become much too friendly with the batman."

"Later, precious," she replies soothingly. "There are all sorts of things that we need to talk about in private. Come in and see how nice the house looks and then we will all have a special tea in the drawing room." She looks up at him and sees that he is frowning. "Perhaps you would you prefer Nanny and the children to have their tea in the kitchen?" He says that he would, and Nan says she will go and arrange this.

After Nan serves tea on the trolley for them, we have our tea in the kitchen. Felicity shuts the door so we will not disturb them although the drawing room is a long, long way from the kitchen. "Now, darlings," Nan says, "I want you to understand that your father is very tired after fighting the War for so many years so you will need to be very quiet, and," she looked at Hugh, "very well behaved. Your father is used to thousands of soldiers doing exactly what he wants them to without question. If you are noisy or badly behaved and anger him you may get into trouble, and we don't want that do we?" She smiles lovingly at us all. Even Hugh looks a bit scared.

"Can I go into the drawing room?" Felicity asks. "I want to tell him more about my exam results."

"No, Felicity, they are busy talking and you must not

disturb them. And another thing," she continues, "you mustn't go into Mummy's bedroom without first knocking on the door and waiting to hear her tell you to come in."

"Why not, Nan?" I ask.

"Because it is good manners to knock first, and your father is very strict about good manners," she replies. "Felicity, please can you help me prepare supper later? Hugh, please fill the coalscuttle for me and when you have done that maybe you would like to work on your coin collection quietly, here in the kitchen, and then you can show it to your father later. Henny, the Little Ones and I are going to play in the nursery until it's their bedtime. Just be quiet and all will be well."

"What about supper?" ask Hugh, who is always hungry.

"I am not sure yet, Hugh, I expect we will have an early supper in here and then your parents can have theirs later."

"What is 'parents'?" I ask.

"Bless my soul!" she replies, "What has the world come to, when, at five years old, you don't know what the word 'parents' means? The War has a lot to answer for." She shakes her head and explains to me that my parents are my mother and my father. "Now you Big Ones, please get on with everything I asked you to do. I'm taking the Little Ones to the nursery."

"I'm not a Little One, Nan, you said I wasn't. I don't want to be a Little One like Lizzybuff and Charlotte," I whine.

"If you are too small to be a Big One, Henny, and too big to be a Little One, what are you?"

"Piggy-in-the-middle!" Hugh chortles. Before I can react, Nan hurries us out of the kitchen and into the nursery.

Chapter 32
The Final Straw

We have not seen our mother or our father very much since he returned because they spend most of the time in their bedroom or the drawing room or taking long walks together. Ted and I stay close to Nan, as we are both still scared of this large stranger.

It is our first meal together as a family since our father's return and Nan has made a very delicious pie from some pigeons Hugh snared and my mother has made a steamed pudding and custard.

Our father asks why we are eating in the kitchen and not in the dining room.

"When we moved into the house there were some problems with the dining room. We use it to store the empty crates and tea chests in and I keep the door locked."

"What sort of problems?"

"I can't remember, there's a big hole in the floor and a problem with the fireplace I think," she replies, uncertainly.

"Why didn't you ask Briggs to fix it?"

"He has been so incredibly busy that I did not think to ask him. We have managed quite well using the kitchen," she replies, "and it was one room less to heat."

Our father snorts and mutters something about getting it fixed and my mother, trying to smooth things over, tells us that our father has brought us some special presents from Africa and that we may open them before tea.

She turns to him and asks him about life in the desert and whether it had changed much in the years since she had lived there. He told her about one of his treks and about some water problems in one of the oases.

"Do you remember our trek to the mountains?" she asks him. "And that I was the first English woman that the people there had ever seen?" she laughs and takes his hand in hers. She gazes into his eyes mistily and he leans over and kisses her. "They were good days, weren't they? Do you remember the fancy dress party at the Officer's Mess?" They laugh together and continue to talk between themselves.

Later our father turns to us and says he has two things to tell us. "Firstly, I do not want my dog referred to as Poor Old Bunker; he is not poor, he is not particularly old and his name is Bunker. Do you understand?"

We tell him that we do and Hugh says he is pleased how happy Bunker is now his master is home again.

"Secondly, starting this Sunday, you three children will attend the church service with me and I expect you all to behave properly," he continues.

"That is a good idea, you will all enjoy that won't you?" We all agree.

Our mother then suggests that we play cricket after tea.

"The bat is broken," Hugh mutters quietly, looking very worried.

"Broken?" booms our father, "Broken? What do you mean, broken? A top quality cricket bat like mine doesn't break. That bat is the one that I played for Bedfordshire with in 1920, absolutely the best that money could buy."

"I had forgotten it was broken, and I cannot remember how that happened," my mother replies vaguely. "Maybe instead, you could all play French cricket," she smiles brightly at us, "with one of the old tennis racquets."

"French cricket!" our father splutters, "that is a game for sissies and girls," contempt rings in his voice, "as soon as we have finished lunch I want you to bring me my cricket bat, Hugo, and I will see," he pauses and frowns at my poor brother, "how it managed to break itself."

The kitchen is suddenly very quiet. Hugh turns very pale and both Nan and my mother look as worried as I feel.

There is going to be a big scene when he finds out what happened to that bat.

The meal continues silently until I clumsily knock over my full glass of orange juice, which spills all over the clean white tablecloth. "Just what I mean," gloats our father, "Look at that! The child has no manners at all."

"It has been difficult, precious," our mother tells him, smiling bravely. "Nanny and I have done our very best but it has not been easy without a man in the house…"

"Briggs is a man," I remark.

"Be quiet, young lady," he roars at me, purple in the face, "Nanny, please remove her to the nursery. She can finish her meal later."

Looking very surprised Nan takes my hand and leads me, sobbing, out of the room and into the nursery.

"What did I say wrong, Nan? Why is he so cross? Doesn't he like us? I don't like him at all."

"Hush, darling, don't ever say anything like that, your Mummy would be very unhappy to hear you say that. She loves him so much…"

"Well, I like Briggs much more than him…"

"Henny, you must not very say that either. That is why you are getting into trouble. Now your father is back Briggs can't be your best friend any more."

"Why not?"

"Because," she says slowly, "instead of being your best friend, he now has to be your father's military servant. He has to look after his uniforms, polish his brass buttons, clean his shoes and keep his dressing room tidy. He is here to be the Colonel's batman, not to play with you."

"I don't understand," I say sadly. Nan, hands me her big white handkerchief to wipe my eyes.

"No, Henny, there's lots of things you won't understand, because you are too young. Listen carefully to what I tell you and you will be all right. Just don't mention Briggs' name again to your father. I think you and I should spend a lot more time together until he settles down. He has had a very hard time being away all these years fighting the War."

"Does fighting the War make people cross?" I ask.

"Yes, Henny, I really think it does. Now, hug Ted tight and make yourselves comfy in the chair by the fire. I'll cover you with Charlotte's shawl and as soon as lunch is finished I'll bring you yours and sit with you whilst you eat it. And," she adds with a smile, "I'll save the whole custard skin for you as a special treat!"

Dear Nan, Ted and I love her so much. We drift off to sleep.

She wakes me up and I see that Charlotte is in the playpen and Lizzybuff in the big wicker chair and that they are both sleeping peacefully, totally unaware of the awful changes that are happening to our family. She sits me up at the table to eat the rest of my lunch. "Nan, what will happen when he sees the bat?"

"I don't know, Henny. Poor Hugh, I am afraid he will get into an awful lot of trouble."

"Will our father kill him?" I ask anxiously.

"No, darling, of course your father won't kill him. Whatever next? You do have such funny ideas in that head of yours. It's the War, I suppose," she adds to herself with a sigh.

"Nan, I'm 'depwessed'."

"Oh! Henny, of course you aren't! It's only Grown-Ups like your mother who get depressed. Perhaps you are just a bit sad and muddled about what's happening and I expect you have tummy ache?" I nod. Now," she continues, soothingly, "I am going to finish knitting Lizzybuff's pink jumper. Why don't you draw a picture of Ted in his best jersey? Later on, we will all go for a walk."

"Nan, will Mother still give me my lessons? Just her and me?"

"We'll have to see about that, Henny, but I shouldn't mention it at the moment because she will want to spend as much time as possible with your father now he is home."

The crackle of the fire and the click of Nan's knitting needles help quieten me down inside and I quickly become involved in drawing Ted and then colouring him, trying very hard to keep inside the lines.

After our walk, we go into the kitchen to get the tea ready. There is a box waiting for me and when I open it I see some silver bracelets and a pretty pair of thin leather slippers with a round pattern on the front. There is also a doll, the most horrible looking one I have ever seen. Betty is ugly but this one is much worse. Her face is pink and made of china with painted blue eyes and very red lips. Her hair is yellow and I can see where it is glued onto her head. I raise her flowered dress to look at her body; it's very hard and covered in cotton material. She had funny round metal things to make her arms and legs move, and the whole doll is stiff and uncomfortable looking. I hate her on sight and decide that she will never come into bed with Ted and me and the others; she can stay in the cold nursery all by herself in the dark, every single night.

"She's horrid," I tell Nan, who is watching me unpack the parcel.

"For goodness sake, Henny, don't tell your father that. Look at the bracelets and the slippers, they are lovely aren't they? I agree. "Well, then, when you thank your father very much for the presents, whatever you do, don't tell him that you think the doll is horrid. If he asks you if you like her you will have to tell a little fib and say you do."

"Why?"

"Because, darling, you have to learn to keep out of trouble. If you don't listen to me and just say what you think, you will get into trouble. And don't ask questions. Things will calm down when your father gets used to being back with the family again and next month he will go back to his office at the barracks at Burdock Coombe and then he will only be here at weekends."

"Now help me lay the trolley for their tea and I will take it into the drawing room and then we will have ours. It's not really a nanny's job to serve tea, but," she smiles at me, "at the moment I'll do anything for the sake of peace and quiet!"

After tea Hugh is summoned to the drawing room with the cricket bat. Nan quietly opens the nursery door a crack so we can hear what is happening. We listen with bated breath.

"Show me, Hugo," our father orders. Hugh must have handed him the bat and the handle because there is dead silence and then the sound of our father letting out his breath. "Well," he growls menacingly, "and what have we here? My top-quality pre-War cricket bat utterly ruined and in two pieces. I shall not be able to win any matches with this now, shall I?"

"Your mother tells me that you have been fighting both on the bus and with the boys in the village. I am very annoyed and disappointed to hear this, Hugo. I can also see that the girls are not as well behaved as they should be. However, you, Hugo," he pauses, "are the worst of the lot."

Hearing this, I wish that I am, just for once, a Little One and too small to get into trouble. I cling to Nan's hand dreading to hear what else he will say.

"Bring Henrietta in here, Nanny, instead of listening at the nursery door," he orders. Both looking a bit pink, we enter the drawing room.

"Hugo, come down to the stable with me and I will show you what happens when you have misbehaved." Hugh looks scared. "Now!" Our father commands. Hugh leaps to his feet.

"Please don't beat him, Colonel," Nan beseeches. "I know he's been naughty but he's been such a help to me, fetching in the coal and …"

"Nanny, I will discipline my children as I see fit until they learn how to behave. Hugo has to learn not to fight and not to ruin other people's property," he replies, holding up the spoiled bat and shaking it to emphasize his point.

They leave the drawing room and she takes me back into the nursery and quietly closes the door.

"Nan, he's going to kill him, I know he is."

"Oh, Henny, of course he isn't. I am sure that your father won't be so cross once he gets used to us all again. And Hugh did leave his special bat out in the rain and it did get badly spoilt and he has been very naughty, so maybe he deserves getting punished."

"I know that he's going to kill him!" I wail.

"No, darling, of course he isn't. And," she adds looking very serious, "if you say that again you will really get into a lot of trouble, not just with your father but with your mother too. Now quieten down and I'll read you a story. Get Ted and come up on my knee even though you really are much too big to sit on your old Nan's knee," she says with a smile. Ted and I cuddle up against her and soon begin to feel better.

"Don't you remember how much you loved your father when he came home for weekends at Burdock Coombe before we moved here?"

I sit bolt upright. "No, I didn't, Nan. You are wrong. I have never, ever seen our father before. Not until we went to meet him at the Bus Station."

"Yes, Henny, you have, of course you have. Don't you remember the fun you had when he used to give you piggyback rides when we went for walks?"

"No, Nan, I don't, and I hope the War will start again and he will have to go away. Then Mother will give me my lessons all by myself and Briggs will be my friend again. If our father doesn't go away, we will run away, won't we Ted?"

I look up at Nan and, seeing the loving look she gives me, I know that we just cannot live without her.

"Nan, will you come with us? Please?"

The End

Post-Script

Apart from the great joy I experience in writing, what was my reason for writing this book?

I loved living at The Old Manor Farmhouse so much that I wanted to record everything I could remember about it and my happy childhood there. When I was twelve years old my parents bought a house in the next county. It was during this move that, sadly, Ted got lost.

Some time later I was travelling on a bus that passed our old property. Expecting it to be as it as it was when we left, I was horrified to see that the house, the barns and the stables had been demolished. All that remained intact was our nursery toy cupboard standing up in a pile of rubble with some of my drawings still pasted to the door.

I felt devastated, as though my very childhood had been demolished. Night after night I used to dream of returning and finding the property as it used to be. Maybe writing this book is my way of rebuilding that wonderful place.

As to our father's return after the War; I have no memory of ever seeing him before the day I met him in October 1945. The picture I had of him was based, on the one hand, on my mother's romantic stories and their obvious great love for each other, and, on the other hand, the stern photos of him in uniform.

My mother's frequently repeated mantra "When the War ends, there will be world Peace and your father will return," led me to expect an amazingly happy, transforming event that would result in us becoming a proper family with a mother and a father and all of us living happily together ever after.

The reality for me, and for many families, was very different.

Our father returned, having commanded thousands of obedient troops in the desert, to a household of four well brought up children. However, our behaviour did not meet with his ingrained military expectations and trouble ensued. I now saw him both in the role of my mother's Beloved and as the severe officer in the photographs.

Having basked in my mother's love and attention through

her teaching me to be an artist she now transferred both to our father, and quite rightly so, but I felt deserted and shut out and resentful that our harmonious family dynamics had been so drastically ripped apart and that my closeness with my mother based on my art lessons had evaporated.

I remember the ensuing era as the most traumatic time of my life and it also coincided with the beginning of my suffering from what I later understood to be depression. Sixty years after the event tears streamed down my face as I wrote the last two chapters of this book.

As an adult I have come to understand why our father, a career officer, was the way he was when he returned from this, his second world war. Not only did he have to deal with the memories of all his wartime experiences but, like all of us, had to adjust to being part of the family after so many years of separation, which was a vast change from his rigid military life.

It was finally our shared love of animals that brought us closer as we cared for the rabbits and all the other animals he added to our ménage and we did eventually establish a good father daughter relationship.

Our parent's love was so strong and enduring that, many, many years later our father, who was elderly but in good health, died of a broken heart just three weeks after our mother's death.